SELLING SMARTER:

Achieve Your Quota, Get Back on Track, & Work Strategically

By Kevin Onarecker

Twin Horseshoes Publishing

www.twinhorseshoes.ca

Ontario, Canada

This publication contains the opinions and ideas of its author and is designed to provide useful information in regard to the subject matter covered. The author and publisher are not engaged in professional services in this publication. This publication is not intended to provide a basis for action in particular circumstances without consideration by a competent professional. The author and publisher expressly disclaim any responsibility for any liability, loss, or risk, personal or otherwise, which is incurred as a consequence, directly or indirectly, of the use and application of any of the contents of this book. While the author has made every effort to provide accurate information at publication time, the publisher and the author assume no responsibility for author or third-party websites or their content.

Onarecker, Kevin

SELLING SMARTER: Achieve Your Quota, Get Back on Track, & Work Strategically

eBook ISBN 979-8-9857924-0-9

Paperback ISBN 979-8-9857924-1-6

Nonfiction | Business & Economics | Development | Business Development

Nonfiction | Business & Economics | Sales & Selling | General

Nonfiction | Business & Economics | Personal Success

DEDICATION

I would like to dedicate this book to the following people:

Mom: Thank you for being my biggest supporter and cheerleader.

Dad: You were my example of how to do everything that is important in life.

My Leaders: Thank you for guiding, encouraging, and challenging me. You inspired me to constantly grow as a professional.

My Teams: Without you, my most cherished and satisfying memories would not have occurred.

Marcia: Thank you for helping me accomplish my dream. This book would not have been completed without you.

My Kids: I am proud of you. Your list of accomplishments is just beginning.

Shasta: You inspire me. You show me unfailing faith and trust. You cry with me and celebrate with me. The person that you are challenges me to be my best, always. Thank you for sharing your life with me. I love you.

TABLE OF CONTENTS

SECTION 4: MAXIMIZING THE PILLARS OF SUCCESS 179

INTRODUCTION

Early in my career I struggled to consistently achieve quota. Frustrated and seeking answers, I went to my manager to get his advice. His suggestion was to "make one more call every day."

It is said the definition of insanity is doing the same thing over and over but expecting different results. My challenge was not that I was not working hard enough, it was that I really did not understand how to succeed consistently as a sales professional. I was unable to achieve my quarterly and annual quota consistently. As my results varied, so did my income along with my sense of professional achievement and satisfaction.

I was highly motivated to learn, grow, and achieve. I wanted to be successful as a sales professional and was willing to work at it. As I progressed, I began to understand how to sell more effectively and what I needed to do to be successful.

As my skills, abilities, and results grew, I moved into roles of greater responsibility. I progressed to field sales trainer and guest trainer at company meetings, to regional sales manager, and ultimately to Vice President of Sales. In those roles I led teams to achieve goals and strategic initiatives. I also helped other sales professionals to grow and develop in their respective careers.

As a sales leader I sold to and negotiated with leadership in customer accounts and key strategic partners. The stakes were always high, so throughout my career my professional skills had to be sharp and current.

Every sales professional goes through the same crucible. That is, every sales professional must learn how to consistently achieve their quota and achieve strategic goals or their career in sales will be short and unrewarding. Every sales professional must continue to grow their skills and abilities because what they must achieve in an advanced role gets more challenging. That is true whether you choose to be a career sales professional or if you choose to take on roles that carry greater responsibility.

My purpose in writing this book is to share insights I have learned in real world selling and business management so that your own learning curve may be shorter, and your professional effectiveness can be maximized. I want you to be able to put the odds of success squarely in your corner, And, to achieve your goals skillfully and consistently such that you overdeliver in what is expected of you, that you may truly enjoy the rewards of a job well done.

Selling Smarter provides you insights, tools, and strategies to achieve and exceed your assigned quota consistently by knowing *what* you need to do to perform at your best. You will be guided to systematically identify *how* to work smarter and more efficiently so that you consistently achieve your goals. If you use *Selling Smarter* as intended, the result will be a playbook – *your* Playbook – that you create. It will be unique to you and focused on ensuring your success.

The following reports and data should be available for you to reference:

- Prior year's territory sales results (baseline sales)
- Prior year's sales by customer
- Year-to-date sales results (if available)
- 3 Month Run-Rate
- Current Month Sales
- Current year's growth objective
- Your Quota
- Rate of growth or decline for your overall market(s) (percentage as well as dollar volume)
- Pipeline Data
    - Total Pipeline value
    - Dollar value and expected close month of each opportunity you have $\geq$75% confidence will close during your current sales year
    - Sales revenue each expected close will contribute to your current year.
- Prior Year's closed business by customer – dollar value and month the new business closed

- Prior Year's lost business by customer - value and month the business was lost
- Targeted Customers (not currently listed in your Pipeline)

Every sales professional is responsible for driving sales revenue, delivering growth, and achieving goals. Those goals include their quota, first and foremost. Far too often sales professionals struggle to *consistently* achieve their assigned quota. According to various sources, between 46% and 57% of sales professionals perform under their quota.[1][2][3]

Achieving quota is not just a one-year expectation, it is the expectation every year. When quota is not achieved, it is costly. It costs bonus and/or commission dollars. Your annual performance review is negatively impacted because achieving quota is your most vital responsibility. And eventually missing quota negatively impacts your career.

Selling Smarter was written to help you take control of your performance and results. ***Selling Smarter*** provides field-proven insights, tools, and strategies to achieve and exceed your assigned quota. You will know exactly *what* you need to do to create a strategic plan, execute that plan, and perform at your best.

Selling Smarter is written in a unique format because there is a specific intended outcome. Each topic that is presented is an essential component in achieving quota and ensuring that you perform at your personal best.

Every topic is impacted by several factors. Those factors are identified, discussed, and then summarized for you. Focus on the key factors that are most applicable and important to your success. Each topic will include an application exercise that enables you to implement key

[1] CSO Insights: The Research Division of Miller Heiman Group. (2018). *Selling in the Age of Ceaseless Change: The 2018-2019 Sales Performance Report*. Retrieved from: http://online.pubhtml5.com/bwdb/ldyb/ldyb.pdf

[2] Hyken, S. (2018, Sept. 2). *57% of Sales Reps Missed Their Quotas Last Year*. Forbes. Retrieved from: https://www.forbes.com/sites/shephyken/2018/09/02/77-of-sales-reps-missed-their-quotas-last-year/?sh=c98f89d52e4b

[3] Martin, S.W. (2013, Dec. 9). *The Twelve Sales Metrics that Matter Most*. Harvard Business Review. Retrieved from: https://hbr.org/2013/12/new-insight-into-key-sales-metrics

takeaways. As you complete each application exercise you systematically identify *how* you will work more strategically and efficiently to achieve your goals. Step-by-step you create *your* Playbook that is unique to you and focused on your success.

The process of building your Playbook involves the use of several tools. The most common tool used throughout is goal setting. We all know the importance of creating and using goals in business. Setting goals and devising an actionable plan to reach our goals is fundamental to performing at the highest level. Goals should be established for every aspect of your business, especially as it pertains to selling and quota attainment.

In **Selling Smarter** you will write out your goals. Why is this? It is because "Vividly describing your goals in written form is strongly associated with goal success, and people who very vividly describe or picture their goals are anywhere from 1.2 to 1.4 times more likely to successfully accomplish their goals" than people who don't.[4]

We will use the **G.O.S.T. Method** of goal setting. The **G.O.S.T. Method** provides a framework for goal setting along with the strategies and tactics that you will implement to accomplish your goals. G.O.S.T. [5]stands for **G**oal, **O**bjective, **S**trategy, and **T**actics.

Once you have chosen your **goal** (what you're trying to achieve), **objectives** can then be identified. Objectives are like rungs on a ladder that lead you to your goal. Objectives include any prerequisites or strategic sub-goals that must be accomplished for the primary goal to be achieved.

Your **strategy** is how you will achieve your objectives and goal. **Tactics** are the daily actions and activities that bring your strategy to life. Tactics are what you do to execute your strategy.

---

[4] Murphy, M. (2018, Apr. 15). *Neuroscience Explains Why You Need To Write Down Your Goals If You Actually Want To Achieve Them*. Forbes. Retrieved from: https://www.forbes.com/sites/markmurphy/2018/04/15/neuroscience-explains-why-you-need-to-write-down-your-goals-if-you-actually-want-to-achieve-them/?sh=599bddbe7905

Let us look at an example of the G.O.S.T. Method in action. Let us say that we want to build a four-bedroom house. Building a house requires many steps, such as starting with a set of blueprints (plans), pouring the foundation, erecting the frame, installing a roof, running electrical and plumbing lines, finishing the interior and exterior surfaces, and much more.

Our G.O.S.T. method for building a four-bedroom house would look like this:

Goal: Build a four-bedroom house

Objectives:

- Create the blueprints
- Pour the foundation
- Erect the frame
- Install the roof
- Run the electrical system
- Install plumbing
- Finish the interior
- Finish the exterior surfaces

Strategies:

- Subcontract each part of the building project
- Oversee and manage the building process

Tactics:

- Hire a general manager
- Meet with GM to sequence and schedule each part of the project
- Review progress and completion of each finished project
- Occupy and enjoy!

Similarly, in selling, we apply the G.O.S.T. Method to identify the sales revenue goal and the objectives that must be achieved to hit that goal. The strategies are <u>how</u> you will accomplish your objectives. The strategies direct your tactics as you put your "feet to the street." Tactics are the actions you take in the daily pursuit of your goals.

So that you can seamlessly use **Selling Smarter** to build your playbook, it is helpful to have some resources at hand. Those resources include:

- Prior year's territory sales results (baseline sales)
- Prior year's sales by customer
- Year-to-date sales results (if available)
- 3-month run-rate
- Current month's sales
- Current year's growth objective
- Your quota
- Rate of growth or decline for your overall market(s) (percentage as well as dollar volume).
- Pipeline data:
  - Total pipeline value.
  - Dollar value and expected close month of each opportunity you have $\geq$75% confidence will close during your current sales year.
  - Sales revenue each expected close will contribute to your current year.
- Prior year's closed business by the customer – dollar value and month the new business closed.
- Prior year's lost business by customer - value and month the business was lost.
- Targeted customers (not currently listed in your pipeline).

SECTION 1: HOW TO ACHIEVE YOUR QUOTA – THE SMART WAY

As a sales professional, you know that achieving quota, and doing so consistently year in and year out is the single biggest challenge you face! Successfully achieving quota requires a diversity of selling skills, interpersonal skills, business acumen, winning strategies, a meticulous plan, and unerring execution. The right attitude and focused effort are required as well. The highest performing sales professionals leverage self-motivation, self-discipline, determination, and good old hard work!

Your professional skills, abilities, and daily activities yield results, which are expressed and reported as a set of numbers. And every sales professional will acknowledge that in the end, it is all about the numbers. Numbers are the language of business.

As a sales professional, your job performance, compensation, and career opportunities are all linked to a very specific set of numbers. Namely, your quota and your quota attainment.

The purpose of *Selling Smarter* is to help you reliably and consistently achieve your sales quota. We do that by identifying each component that is essential in achieving quota and a detailed understanding of what is required for you to achieve your quota. Then following a step-by-step guide, you will systematically construct a detailed plan, resulting in your personal playbook for accomplishing your goals.

Section Goals

- **Accurately determine the sales revenue growth required to achieve your quota.**
- **Identify your <u>best</u> sales revenue growth opportunities.**
- **Craft your strategic plan to grow sales revenue and achieve your quota.**

Chapter 1: The Numbers that Impact Quota Attainment

Let us start by focusing on your quota. There are three parts to the quota equation. Those parts are baseline sales (your territory's prior year (PY) total sales revenue), the growth objective, and the resulting figure, which is the quota. The quota equation can be expressed in a few ways:

Baseline Sales + Growth Objective = Quota

Or

Quota - Baseline Sales = Growth Objective

To ensure you achieve your quota, or better yet exceed it, you need an effective plan. An effective plan is comprised of goals, objectives, strategy, and tactics. Your goal is your quota. There may be other strategic goals or initiatives that you are responsible for. If you have goals in addition to your quota you will need to construct a plan to achieve them as well.

Achieving quota requires a specific volume of new sales revenue generation. While the quota equation is simple to understand, there are often underlying revenue dynamics in your territory that add complexity and variability.

By understanding those underlying dynamics and how they impact your territory's sales revenue you can determine an accurate volume of sales revenue growth needed for you to achieve quota. That enables you to accurately account for them in your strategic planning.

Dynamics You Must Understand

Some products are purchased frequently and routinely such as monthly subscriptions or the "razorblades" in a razor/razorblade model that are purchased in recurring monthly quantities. Other products are purchased with less frequency but are still purchased in relatively consistent patterns, such as quarterly. Still, other products are purchased only once every few years, such as automobiles or capital equipment.

Depending on the nature of your product(s) and the frequency and consistency with which they are purchased, some or all the factors listed below will impact your territory's baseline sales revenue, its underlying dynamics, the sales revenue growth required to achieve quota, and ultimately, your ability to achieve quota.

- Baseline sales.
- Sales revenue run rate.
- Growth objective and net growth objective.
- Total market's rate of growth/decline within your territory.
- Customers exhibiting sales revenue growth or decline.
- Positive and negative carry forward.
- Sales pipeline:
  - Value of opportunities.
  - Timing of projected closes and when revenue is captured in your sales reports.
- The volume of closed new business.

Let us take a closer look at each factor. As we review them consider how each factor impacts your territory's sales revenue and how you will account for those factors as you begin to construct your strategic plan.

Baseline Sales

The prior year's (PY) total sales revenue is also known as baseline sales. As we just saw in the quota equation, the sales revenue growth objective is added to your baseline sales to determine your quota. It can be tempting to think that if your growth objective is achieved, then your quota will be achieved as well. Unfortunately, that is not always true.

What is often not factored into the equation is the prior year's sales rate of growth or decline. The rate at which baseline sales are growing or shrinking can make your growth objective relatively easier or relatively more difficult to achieve. Therefore, the rate at which your baseline sales are either growing or shrinking is vital for you to understand, and account for in your planning, so you can calculate the net sales revenue growth (net growth objective) needed to achieve your quota.

Sales Revenue Run Rate

To better understand the underlying trends, review your territory's 12-month and 3-month rate of growth or decline measured in dollars and percentage change.

- Your 12-month sales revenue run rate and rate of change is measured over the most recent 12-month period. This is typically at the beginning of the new sales year but can be done for any 12-month period you wish to analyze.
  - Example: If your total sales revenue grew from $1,300,000 to $1,500,000 over the most recent 12 months, your rate of growth was 15.4% and +$200,000 for the period.
- Your 3-month sales revenue run rate and rate of change is measured in the same way over the most recent 3-month period. Your 3-month run rate is the more current measure of your sales trends and often differs slightly from your 12-month run rate.

By calculating and comparing the 12-month and 3-month run rates, you will have a clearer understanding of the rate of change within your territory's baseline sales and whether that change is accelerating, remaining unchanged, or slowing. These measures may also be referred to as sales revenue trends.

If the 3-month rate of change is greater than the 12-month rate of change then the sales revenue trend is accelerating. The opposite is true as well.

How should you use the sales trend analysis data? Let us review three scenarios and the implications of each.

Scenario 1: Prior Year (PY) sales were growing at the rate of 10% year over year. If the PY total annual sales (baseline sales) were $1M then barring other changes, the territory would be projected to achieve approximately $1.1M in annual sales for the current year (CY).

Scenario 2: PY sales were flat - neither growing nor declining. If the PY total annual sales were $1M then barring other changes, the territory would be projected to achieve approximately $1M in annual sales for the CY.

Scenario 3: PY sales were declining at the rate of 10% year over year. If PY total annual sales were $1M then barring other changes, the territory would be projected to achieve only $900K in annual sales for the CY.

Let us assume the rate of growth or decline in baseline sales was not considered when the growth objective and quota was assigned for the current year. Each territory was assigned a growth objective of $100K, or +10% over baseline sales. The quota formula for all three territories would be:

Baseline Sales of $1,000,000 + Growth Objective of $100,000 = Quota of $1,100,000.

However, the reality is that each scenario would require dramatically different sales revenue growth results to achieve the assigned quota. To see this, let us make two assumptions: 1) the underlying sales trend for each scenario continues at the same rate through the current year and 2) $100,000 of new sales revenue growth occurs in each scenario that is in addition to any growth or decline due to the underlying sales trend.

Following the assumptions above, annual sales for each scenario would be as follows:

Scenario 1: $1,000,000 baseline sales + (+10% rate of underlying sales trend growth = $100,000) + $100,000 new sales revenue growth = $1,200,000 total sales revenue.

Scenario 2: $1,000,000 baseline sales + (0% rate of underlying sales trend growth = $0) + $100,000 new sales revenue growth = $1,100,000 total sales revenue.

Scenario 3: $1,000,000 baseline sales + (-10% rate underlying sales trend decline = -$100,000) + $100,000 new sales revenue growth = $1,000,000 total sales revenue.

You can see how important it is for you to understand the rate of growth or rate of decline in your baseline sales! Dig into your sales reports and know your trends because that trend will need to be accounted for in your plan to achieve quota!

Growth Objective and Net Growth Objective

As we have just seen, there are really two growth objectives. The first growth objective is the one added to baseline sales to calculate quota. In our previous example, that growth objective was $100,000.

The second growth objective is the _net_ growth objective. The net growth objective is determined by taking into account the rate of growth or decline in your baseline sales and/or current sales trend and adding that to your assigned growth objective. _The net growth objective is what you must generate to achieve your quota._

Figure 1.1

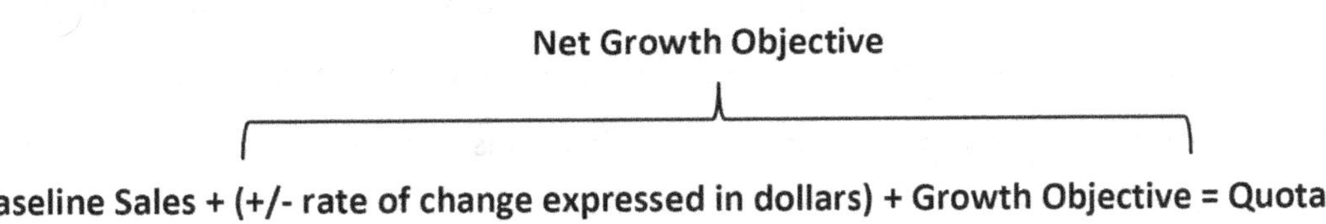

Scenario 1: $1,000,000 + (10% growth rate = $100,000) + $100,000 sales revenue growth = $1,200,000

If we reexamine Scenario 1, we see that the **net growth objective** is $0. That is because when the 10% rate of growth is applied to the $1M baseline sales it will provide the $100,000 growth you are being asked to generate.

If you also gain an additional $100,000 in new sales revenue, that growth will enable you to exceed your annual quota by that amount because your total sales will be approximately $1,200,000!

Scenario 2: $1,000,000 + (0% growth rate = $0) + $100,000 sales revenue growth = $1,100,000

In Scenario 2, there is a 0% growth rate so you cannot expect to gain any sales revenue dollars from pre-existing growth. Your net growth objective is $100,000. That is the net growth required over the sales baseline to achieve your quota of $1,100,000.

Scenario 3: $1,000,000 + (-10% growth rate = -$100,000) + $100,000 sales revenue growth = $1,000,000

In Scenario 3 you must generate $200,000 in net sales revenue growth to achieve quota. That "extra" growth is required due to the erosion of baseline sales. That is, the -10% rate of change to $1,000,000 baseline sales will cause a projected loss of $100,000 during the current year. That must be made up for <u>and</u> the assigned $100,000 growth objective must be generated to achieve quota. Therefore, the net growth objective is $200,000.

Now, a few words to the wise! First, remember that in these examples we assumed that the underlying sales momentum for each scenario would continue at the same rate through the current year. Like other assumptions, that is rarely the case. For your planning purposes, you must understand your baseline sales trends. But be aware that you will need to continuously monitor monthly sales reports to stay abreast of any changes in trends and account for them through the course of the year.

Secondly, suppose you find yourself in a position like Scenario 1 where your sales trends suggest that your net growth objective is very small, or even $0! What a wonderful place to be, correct? Yes, it is terrific to have strong sales momentum but do NOT assume that you can just sit back and relax or that you won't have to grow additional sales revenue.

Trends can and do change. Enjoy the sales "tailwinds" but strive to close new business continuously, as if you did not have the growth trend providing the additional sales revenue. By doing so you maximize your performance and earnings in the current sales year. You also keep the trends and the momentum in your favor. Positive carry forward sets the stage for success in the following year.

Total Market's Rate of Growth or Decline

It is said that a rising tide lifts all boats. If your product's market is growing, then you can experience sales revenue growth even when your product's market share does not change. Sales revenue growth can be easier to generate if the market is growing because either there are more potential customers, customers are purchasing more of the products that comprise your market, or a combination of both.

If your product's market is stable or shrinking you will need to capture more market share and/or expand your market to grow sales revenue.

Stay abreast of your market trends and understand how those trends may impact your sales revenue potential so that you can plan accordingly.

Customers Exhibiting Sales Revenue Growth or Decline

The sales revenue generated by your existing customers rarely stays the same year over year. Each customer typically purchases either more of your product, or less of your product, when compared to their prior year purchases. It is important to know the number of customers who are purchasing more of your product versus the number of those purchasing less of your product. It is also important to know the volume of sales revenue for each customer that is either growing or declining. The difference of cumulative revenue growth versus decline will determine the overall revenue growth or decline for your territory.

To understand and predict sales revenue growth or decline at the territory level, you must understand what is driving high volume sales revenue growth or decline for your customers. To be clear, we are not talking about customers that are newly acquired. Sales revenue growth from new customers is self-explanatory. Your focus should be on understanding what is now, or may be in the future, causing large volume sales revenue changes within your current base of customers.

Your customers have business factors that impact them, which will ultimately impact how much of your product or service they purchase. In short, if your customer's business is growing then your business with them may grow as well. If your customer's business is in decline, then the amount of product they purchase from you is likely to decline as well.

If a customer's purchases have fallen off, yet their business is otherwise healthy, you need to investigate to understand why the changes are occurring. You may be under competitive threat, or your customer may be changing how or why they use your product.

To best understand current customers and the associated sales revenue, you must understand their typical product purchase timing and volume. This is especially true for your large, key customers. By knowing customer purchase patterns, you can understand when sales revenues are truly growing or declining versus exhibiting change solely due to a variance in the timing of their purchases.

Positive and Negative Carry Forward

Positive and negative carry forward will impact your sales revenue trends if your customers purchase your products in a regular, recurring monthly pattern. Examples of such purchasing patterns include products that are purchased as monthly subscriptions or products that are the disposable "razorblade" in a razor/razorblade product model. If your products are purchased in a regular, recurring monthly pattern, then you need to understand how positive and negative carry forward impact your territory's sales revenue.

With such products, when new business is generated, the resulting new sales revenue is reflected in your sales reports as growth over baseline (PY) sales for twelve months. Beginning with the thirteenth month, the sales revenue resulting from the original sale no longer provides growth over baseline sales. That is because the revenue from the original close has now become part of baseline sales.

See Figure 1.2. In the example, Year 1 Monthly Sales are the baseline sales that Year 2 Monthly Sales are being compared to. In February of Year 2, new business is closed, providing $20,000 in new sales revenue each month going forward. Barring other losses or gains, the monthly sales revenue will grow from $100,000 to $120,000. For the remainder of Year 2, each month will show growth of $20,000 when compared to the same month in Year 1. A total of $220,000 in annual sales revenue growth will have occurred when compared to the prior year (baseline sales).

In January, Year 3 begins (Figure 1.3). The monthly sales from Year 2 now become the baseline sales that Year 3 sales are compared to. Notice that in February of Year 3 the monthly sales and the Year 2 monthly sales are both $120,000. That means no revenue growth has occurred when Feb Y3 is compared to Feb Y2. Barring other losses or gains, the same will be true for every month of Year 3. The total annual sales revenue growth over baseline in Year 3 will be $20,000.

The same carry forward concept applies to any losses that occur. Lost business and the associated sales revenue "bleeds out" each month for twelve months and after that, the lost sales are no longer part of baseline sales. It is important to understand that although the losses will no longer impact each month going forward, the baseline will be permanently lower if no new customers are added to offset the loss.

Unless the new business sales revenue is gained (or sales revenue loss occurs) in the first month of your fiscal year, the twelve months of positive or negative impact affect two fiscal years. In the example above you can see that Year 2 and Year 3 were both impacted.

To illustrate again how this happens, the shaded line in the example below represents new business sales revenue gained. Notice that new sales revenue contributes growth over baseline sales from March through December in the *current year*. Then, for the first two months of the following sales year, you will also enjoy additional sales revenue growth over baseline sales. The two months of additional new sales revenue over baseline sales is the positive <u>carry forward</u>.

Then, in the thirteenth month (in this example the thirteenth month is March of the second year), those monthly gains become part of your baseline sales just like in our first example. Though your customer continues to purchase their normal monthly amount it no longer is revenue growth over baseline sales.

Figure 1.2

Close Occurs, adding $20,000 in new sales revenue each month

	Jan	Feb	Mar	Apr	May	Jun	Jul	Aug	Sep	Oct	Nov	Dec
Yr 2 Monthly Sales	$ 100,000	$ 120,000	$ 120,000	$ 120,000	$ 120,000	$ 120,000	$ 120,000	$ 120,000	$ 120,000	$ 120,000	$ 120,000	$ 120,000
Yr 1 Monthly Sales	$ 100,000	$ 100,000	$ 100,000	$ 100,000	$ 100,000	$ 100,000	$ 100,000	$ 100,000	$ 100,000	$ 100,000	$ 100,000	$ 100,000
Growth (Yr2 vs Yr1)	$ -	$ 20,000	$ 20,000	$ 20,000	$ 20,000	$ 20,000	$ 20,000	$ 20,000	$ 20,000	$ 20,000	$ 20,000	$ 20,000

Figure 1.3

Close Occurs, adding $20,000 in new sales revenue each month

	Jan	Feb	Mar	Apr	May	Jun	Jul	Aug	Sep	Oct	Nov	Dec
Yr 3 Monthly Sales	$ 120,000	$ 120,000	$ 120,000	$ 120,000	$ 120,000	$ 120,000	$ 120,000	$ 120,000	$ 120,000	$ 120,000	$ 120,000	$ 120,000
Yr 2 Monthly Sales	$ 100,000	$ 120,000	$ 120,000	$ 120,000	$ 120,000	$ 120,000	$ 120,000	$ 120,000	$ 120,000	$ 120,000	$ 120,000	$ 120,000
Growth (Yr3 vs Yr2)	$ 20,000	$ -	$ -	$ -	$ -	$ -	$ -	$ -	$ -	$ -	$ -	$ -

Figure 1.4

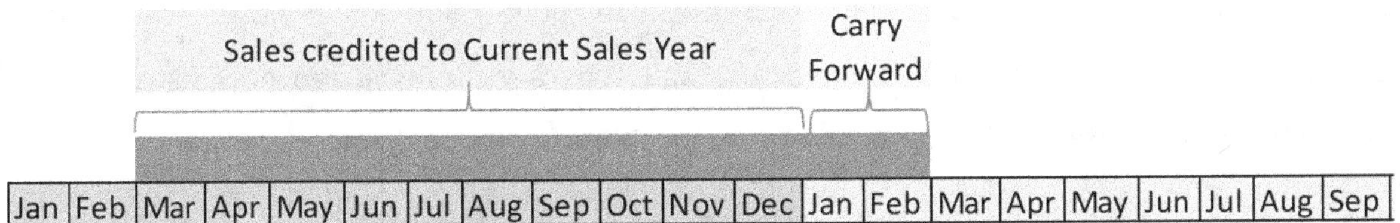

While this example is for new sales revenue, which provides a positive impact going forward, the reverse situation occurs when a customer is lost. In that case, whatever monthly sales were generated by the customer will NOT occur going forward, so over twelve months, you will have a monthly negative impact of lost sales when compared to baseline sales. Just like new business provides positive carry forward, any lost accounts that stop purchasing within your current sales year will cause negative carry forward that will negatively impact the next sales year. Refer to your sales reports to see exactly what the total impact of lost customers will be.

To project a positive carry forward impact, consider the closes that occurred in your territory. What month did the close occur? What was the average monthly new sales revenue that resulted? Multiply the average monthly revenue by the number of months of carry forward to project the sales revenue growth you may expect in the coming year.

Sales Pipeline

The sales pipeline will be discussed much more later in the book. As it pertains to your ability to achieve quota, your pipeline has two very important metrics. First, there must be enough new sales revenue potential in your pipeline to achieve the required sales revenue growth (your Net Growth Objective). Second, the opportunity must close soon enough to generate the new sales revenue that is needed. That sales revenue must be received by your organization and reflected in your sales reports sufficient to achieve quota.

As an example, let us say that you need $200,000 in sales revenue growth (Net Growth Objective) to achieve quota. Because not every pipeline opportunity will close, and some opportunities will close later than expected, it is recommended to build in a safety margin of three to four times what you need in new sales revenue. That means if you require $200,000 in sales revenue growth to achieve your quota, your pipeline should have $600,000 - $800,000 in closeable new sales opportunities. Those opportunities must close and generate the expected new sales revenue within the appropriate timeframe for you to capture the revenue and achieve quota.

If your pipeline does not have the needed potential new sales revenue, or if the opportunities will not close quickly enough then your pipeline needs attention. Either you must add more opportunities, or you must advance your opportunities faster, or both. Without these pipeline developments, you will not be able to achieve quota, so this is a vital dynamic to manage!

The Volume of Closed New Business

Every sales professional has heard about the ABCs of closing (Always Be Closing). In this context, to achieve quota your focus must be on always closing enough opportunities that will provide enough sales revenue. "Enough" means the new business opportunities that you close provides the new sales revenue that meets your net growth objective so that you achieve your quota.

Other Factors

Periodically you will have other factors that will impact your territory's sales revenues. These factors may or may not be expected or predictable, and they may not have much data available with which to plan.

One such factor is new product launches. If you are launching a new product you will need to project the expected revenue impact from the sale of that product. Consider whether revenue from the new product will be additive or if new product sales will cannibalize sales from an existing product. If it is a competitive product launch determine how much risk is posed to you and adjust your plan accordingly.

At times new competitors change market dynamics and when they occur, those changes can be substantial. A new competitor can bring new products into the market and/or they can bring changes in business practices. Research as much as you can to ascertain what changes will occur and how your sales revenue and sales revenue growth potential might be impacted.

Customers change as well. New customers may move into your territory or existing customers may leave. The key is to stay abreast of industry and company news so that you can account for any potential gains or losses as quickly as possible. Then you can make and implement your plans to the best advantage.

When you become aware of factors such as these, do the best you can to project the impact on baseline sales and your sales revenue growth potential. Adjust your plan as needed strategically and tactically.

Application: Numbers that Determine Quota Attainment Worksheet

Factors that impact quota attainment are listed below. Using your reports and available data, input the information below.

NOTE: if you have multiple sales goals complete this exercise for each, as necessary.

Your Quota Equation

- Baseline Sales

  $______________

- Growth Objective

  +$______________

- **Quota**

  =$______________

Now, consider any other dynamics that may impact your territory sales revenue. Calculate the expected impact only for those factors that apply to you. Start with the quota figure from above. Add or subtract the anticipated impact of the indicated factors that apply to your territory.

"Other" factors may include new product launches, new competitors, or any factors that you expect to have a measurable positive or negative impact on sales revenue that were not otherwise accounted for.

Determine the <u>net growth objective</u> required to achieve your quota.

____

____

____

____

Territory Sales Dynamics (select and calculate the factors that apply)

- **Quota** (transfer down from above)

    $_____________

- Baseline Sales (X) Rate of growth/decline (percentage) = projected annual sales

    (-)$_____________

- Baseline Sales (X) Market rate of growth/decline = projected impact on sales

    +/-$_____________

- Baseline Sales (X) Current Customer growth/decline = projected impact on sales

    +/-$_____________

- Rule of 78s implications

    o   Positive Carry Forward (for new customers)

        -$_____________

    o   Negative Carry Forward (for lost customers)

        +$_____________

- Other Factors (new product launch, new competitors, etc.)

    +/-$_____________

Projected net sales revenue needed to achieve quota

    =$_____________

NOTE: Dynamics that will positively impact your sales revenue should be subtracted from your quota. Those dynamics that negatively impact your sales revenue should be added to your quota.

____

____

____

____

Quota Attainment – Baseline Sales Run Rate, Market Growth or Decline, Current Customer Growth or Decline, and Positive or Negative Carry Forward from new or lost customers – which of these factors most impact your territory, and what are the implications for your planning?

____

____

____

____

____

____

____

Quota Attainment – Projected net sales revenue growth required to achieve quota – Does this new projected growth figure differ from the simple calculation you started with? If so, how does it impact your plan to attain quota?

____

____

____

____

____

____

____

Chapter 2: Determine Your Monthly Sales Revenue Goals

Now that you have identified your annual quota and your net growth objective, the next step is to create your monthly sales revenue goals. Establishing monthly sales revenue goals allows you to know exactly what you need to generate in new sales revenue each month to achieve your quota. Monthly sales revenue goals also provide a mechanism, a key performance indicator (KPI) to track your performance each month and know if you are on pace to achieve your quota or if adjustments are needed.

How you determine your monthly new sales revenue goals will depend on the nature of your products and how they are purchased.

Monthly New Sales Revenue Goal: Products with Recurring Monthly Sales

For products with recurring monthly sales, use the **Rule of 78s** (Figure 2.1). The Rule of 78s is illustrated in the chart below. Each "X" indicates a purchasing period. Over twelve months there are 78 purchasing periods. As the year progresses, the number of periods remaining decreases as each month goes by. You can see the number of purchasing periods remaining for each month in the far-right column below.

To calculate the monthly new sales revenue required to achieve your year-end quota, focus on your **YTD net growth objective**. That is, how much revenue growth is required over YTD sales to achieve quota?

Here is an example using a growth objective of $272,000 (Figure 2.2). At the beginning of the fiscal year (January in this example), there are 78 purchasing periods. Divide $272,000 by 78. From this calculation, you can see that by closing $3,487 in recurring sales revenue <u>each month</u>, you will generate the required growth of $272,000 and achieve your goal.

Figure 2.1

	Jan	Feb	Mar	Apr	May	Jun	Jul	Aug	Sep	Oct	Nov	Dec	# Periods
Jan	X	X	X	X	X	X	X	X	X	X	X	X	78
Feb		X	X	X	X	X	X	X	X	X	X	X	66
Mar			X	X	X	X	X	X	X	X	X	X	55
Apr				X	X	X	X	X	X	X	X	X	45
May					X	X	X	X	X	X	X	X	36
Jun						X	X	X	X	X	X	X	28
Jul							X	X	X	X	X	X	21
Aug								X	X	X	X	X	15
Sep									X	X	X	X	10
Oct										X	X	X	6
Nov											X	X	3
Dec												X	1

Figure 2.2

	Jan	Feb	Mar	Apr	May	Jun	Jul	Aug	Sep	Oct	Nov	Dec	Totals	# Periods
Monthly Close Goal	$3,487	$3,487	$3,487	$3,487	$3,487	$3,487	$3,487	$3,487	$3,487	$3,487	$3,487	$3,487	**$41,846**	78
	Feb	$3,487	$3,487	$3,487	$3,487	$3,487	$3,487	$3,487	$3,487	$3,487	$3,487	$3,487	**$38,359**	66
		Mar	$3,487	$3,487	$3,487	$3,487	$3,487	$3,487	$3,487	$3,487	$3,487	$3,487	**$34,872**	55
			Apr	$3,487	$3,487	$3,487	$3,487	$3,487	$3,487	$3,487	$3,487	$3,487	**$31,385**	45
				May	$3,487	$3,487	$3,487	$3,487	$3,487	$3,487	$3,487	$3,487	**$27,897**	36
					Jun	$3,487	$3,487	$3,487	$3,487	$3,487	$3,487	$3,487	**$24,410**	28
						Jul	$3,487	$3,487	$3,487	$3,487	$3,487	$3,487	**$20,923**	21
							Aug	$3,487	$3,487	$3,487	$3,487	$3,487	**$17,436**	15
								Sep	$3,487	$3,487	$3,487	$3,487	**$13,949**	10
									Oct	$3,487	$3,487	$3,487	**$10,462**	6
										Nov	$3,487	$3,487	**$6,974**	3
											Dec	$3,487	**$3,487**	1

Total **$272,000**

Application: Use the Rule of 78s to Calculate your Monthly New Sales Revenue Goal

1) Using the Rule of 78s formula in the **first month of your fiscal year**, the formula is as follows:

   Annual net growth objective / 78 = monthly new sales revenue goal.

   Calculate the following using your Net Growth Objective:

   Net Growth Objective $____________ / 78 = Monthly New Sales Revenue Goal $____________

2) You can use the Rule of 78s to update your monthly new sales revenue goal at **any time during the year.** To calculate the monthly new sales revenue required to achieve your year-end quota, focus on your **YTD growth objective**. That is, how much revenue growth remains over YTD sales to achieve quota?

   YTD Growth Objective $____________ / (number of periods remaining) = Monthly New Sales Revenue Goal $____________

NOTE: Know when sales revenues will be received, recorded, and reflected in your sales reports! If a close that occurs in one month will not be reflected in your sales reports until the following month then you must adjust your Rule of 78s calculation accordingly. That is, use the following month (and the associated number of periods remaining) to make your calculations.

Notes:

____

____

____

<u>Application: Calculate non-Recurring New Sales Revenue Goal</u>

Monthly Sales Revenue Goal: Products with Non-recurring Sales

For products that are purchased in <u>non-recurring transactions</u>, the monthly sales revenue goal is calculated as follows: annual quota / 12 = monthly sales revenue goal.

Calculate the following using your Annual Quota:

Annual Quota $___________ / 12 = Monthly Sales Revenue Goal $_______________

To update you create a monthly sales revenue goal through the course of the year, simply divide your remaining quota by the number of months remaining in the year.

NOTE: Know when sales revenues will be received, recorded, and reflected in your sales reports! If a close that occurs in one month will not be reflected in your sales reports until the following month then you must adjust your calculation accordingly. That is, use the following month to make your calculations.

For example, if your remaining annual quota is $100,000 and you have 7 months left in the year, you would use the following calculation: $100,000 / 7 = $14,286. This confirms your monthly goal is to sell an average of $14,286 each month to achieve your quota.

Whether you are selling products with recurring sales patterns or non-recurring transactions, it is necessary to update your monthly goals each month. In doing so, your monthly revenue goals will be clear, accurate, and always up to date.

____

____

____

Chapter 3: Analyze Your Sales Pipeline

Now that you identified the annual sales revenue growth needed to achieve your quota, and your monthly sales revenue goals, you need to determine if your pipeline of opportunities is sufficient to meet your goals.

A Healthy Sales Pipeline

A **healthy pipeline** was previously defined as having *realistic, qualified, and quantified* opportunities with new sales revenue potential totaling at least three to four times the sales revenue growth needed to achieve your goals. **AND** the *timeline* for closing the respective pipeline opportunities ensures the revenue from the closed pipeline opportunities will be received soon enough for you to achieve quota.

Why is it that you should overbuild your pipeline by three to four times the sales revenue growth needed to achieve your goals? It is because not every opportunity will close and those that do won't always close as soon as you expect or need them to. Overbuild your pipeline so that your success does suffer if one or more opportunities don't close or if they fail to close when you expect them to.

The criteria that your pipeline opportunities provide sufficient revenue potential and close within the required timeframe apply to both your monthly goals and your annual goal. If your current pipeline does not meet these criteria, then your pipeline must be further developed until it meets both criteria.

Your pipeline may require the addition of new opportunities and/or progressing existing opportunities through your sales cycle to closure sooner.

Application: Pipeline Analysis

Review your pipeline of opportunities. Ensure that your pipeline meets the revenue and time criteria.

For this review only consider those opportunities that you have a high level of confidence ($\geq$75%) of closing each month and for the current year. By including only those opportunities that you have high confidence in ensures you are not projecting sales revenue from opportunities that are not yet well-developed. The purpose of the pipeline review is to project what you can reasonably expect for new sales revenue as a result of closed opportunities in the coming months, and your total for the year.

When you perform your pipeline review you may not have accurate visibility beyond the next few months. That is okay, work with what you have at present with the knowledge that you will continue to add to your pipeline and develop opportunities throughout the year.

You should have very good visibility for closes you expect to occur within the next few coming months. For this exercise focus on them and any other high-confidence opportunities through yearend.

For non-recurring purchases indicate the full amount of the purchase in the appropriate month. For products with recurring monthly purchases indicate only the monthly value. The expected annual value of such a close can then be projected by multiplying the expected monthly revenue by the number of months remaining in the fiscal year. Do this to understand the revenue you expect to generate monthly and for your current sales year.

Here is a sample pipeline and the revenue projections (Figure 3.1). If you already have a standard pipeline tool or template, use it. If you do not have a template, use the following template for your calculations and review (Figure 3.2).

Figure 3.1

Pipeline Opportunities ≥ 75% Confidence

Name	Product(s)	Close Month	Non-recurring Sales Revenue	Monthly Recurring Sales Revenue	Months of Recurring Reveue	CY Periodic Sales Revenue	Total Sales Revenue
Customer 1	Non-recurring	January	$10,000	$0		$0	$10,000
Customer 2	Mixed	January	$7,500	$2,500	12	$30,000	$37,500
Customer 3	Monthly Recurring	January		$2,100	12	$25,200	$25,200
Customer 4	Monthly Recurring	February		$3,500	11	$38,500	$38,500
Customer 5	Monthly Recurring	February	$1,000	$1,500	11	$16,500	$17,500
Customer 6	Non-recurring	March	$8,000			$0	$8,000
Customer 7	Monthly Recurring	June	$0	$4,500	6	$27,000	$27,000
Customer 8	Non-recurring	September	$5,000			$0	$5,000

Totals: $31,500 $137,200 $168,700

Figure 3.2

Pipeline Opportunities $\geq$ 75% Confidence

Name	Product(s)	Close Month	Non-recurring Sales Revenue	Monthly Recurring Sales Revenue	Months of Recurring Reveue	CY Periodic Sales Revenue	Total Sales Revenue

Totals:

Pipeline Review. Fill in the blanks below. In the monthly column provide the total sales revenue you expect to gain from your current pipeline of opportunities. Provide the sum of non-recurring sales and recurring sales. Then, compare the revenue you expect to gain to the revised monthly close goal you previously identified.

Do the same calculations for your annual totals.

Total $ value of Pipeline $\geq$75% Confidence:	Monthly	Annual
Non-Recurring Sales	$_____________	$_____________
Recurring Sales	+ $_____________	+ $_____________
Expected $ Growth	= $_____________	= $_____________
Net Growth required to achieve quota	$_____________	$_____________

Does your current pipeline provide enough **new sales revenue volume** to sufficiently meet your monthly and annual growth objectives? Will your opportunities **close soon enough,** within the current month and the sales year, to achieve monthly close goals and annual quota? **Yes / No**

If not, how will you develop your pipeline so that it provides sufficient revenue on time for you to achieve quota?

____

____

____

____

____

NOTE: if you have multiple products and/or services each with its quota, you will need to do this same pipeline review for each. Pipeline templates are available in the appendix.

Notes:

Chapter 4: Manage Your Key Customers

Achieving quota requires sales revenue growth. The key question is how much sales revenue growth will be required and what can be done to manage that number? Since sales growth builds upon prior year sales (baseline sales) maintaining your territory's current sales revenue volume is imperative.

Maintain Baseline Sales Volume

Recalling the Net Growth Objective concepts we discussed, we know that any negative impact on baseline sales will make the goal of achieving quota more challenging because we will have to create even more new sales revenue to overcome whatever is causing the negative impact. Some factors that negatively impact baseline sales are not controllable, such as industry trends, new competitors, or new competitive products.

Other factors are controllable and to the best of your ability, you must ensure that you limit or eliminate any losses to your baseline sales. One of the most important ways to avoid negative baseline sales repercussions is to protect your key customers and the business they provide.

The Leaky Bucket

If key customers are lost, additional sales volume will have to be generated sufficient to outweigh any sales revenue losses before net growth can be realized. Having to close new business just to recoup losses is akin to trying to fill a bucket full of holes with water. You continually fill the bucket only to see it drain away the moment you stop. It is far easier and more effective to prevent leakage in the first place.

Example: Let us suppose your territory's baseline sales are $2,000,000. Your sales revenue growth objective is $200,000, so by yearend, you are expected to have generated a total of $2,200,000 of sales revenue.

Baseline Sales + Growth Objective = Quota   **$2,000,000 + $200,000 = $2,200,000.**

If one of your key customers purchased $100,000 of your product in the prior year, that business is part of your territory's $2,000,000 baseline sales. Unfortunately, the customer in question has decided to go to your competition. Since the customer is lost and will not be purchasing from you, their $100,000 in business must be replaced by other customers before any <u>net</u> revenue growth will occur within your territory.

Here is the new equation: $2,000,000 - $100,000 (loss) + $300,000 (growth) = $2,200,000 (quota).

Do you see how your net growth objective just went from $200,000 to $300,00 due to the lost customer? Your net growth objective just increased 50%! That is why key customers are so important to retain and protect!

Key Customers Retention

We have established the importance of retaining and protecting key customers because of the impact they have on your territory's sales revenue and quota attainment. To retain and protect key customers you must first identify who your key customers are. What will be your rationale for classifying them as key customers? What metrics will be used to separate key customers from those who are not key customers?

Identify and Prioritize Your Key Customers

There is more than one methodology and rationale for classifying a customer as a key customer. Some considerations may include the customer's current volume of business, the potential for additional business and revenue generation, influence, thought leadership, geographical location, or even the importance of retaining longstanding affiliations.

One criterion I highly recommend you use to identify key customers is their contribution to your territory's baseline sales. That is because one of the most important reasons to retain and protect key customers is to protect your baseline sales volume. Most of your baseline sales volume can and usually does come from a relative handful of customers.

I am sure you are familiar with the Pareto Principle, also known as the 80/20 Rule. That principle indicates 80% of your business comes from 20% of your customers.[6] When you review your sales reports you will likely see this principle is true for your territory.

I prefer to use a modified version of this principle to identify key customers. I identify those customers who collectively generated 60% of the territory sales revenue. By setting the threshold as those who collectively provide 60% of the territory's revenue, each one of the customers that appear on that list contributes sales revenue that is well worth your time and energy to protect. They are truly your key customers when using sales revenue contribution as the measure.

When you run the analysis for your territory, you are likely to find that group of key customers is much smaller than you might have expected. And, when you see the total dollars and percentage of revenue each key customer contributes to your territory, the need to protect each one becomes obvious. A single loss from this group of customers will negatively impact your territory by 2% to 10+% each. Each one will create big leaks in your bucket if they are lost!

The priority is to protect those key customers and ensure they continue to produce revenue in your territory. An important secondary priority for key customers is to grow their business. Even though key customers already do a large volume of business many of them have the potential to do even more. Don't overlook this source of sales revenue growth.

Now that you have identified who your key customers are let us discuss how to retain them now, and into the foreseeable future.

Know Why Your Key Customers Are Your Customer

To retain key customers, it is important to understand three important things: (1) why they became your customer in the first place. And (2) why they are your customer presently. Most

---

[6] Juran. (2019, Mar. 12). *Pareto Principle (80/20 Rule) & Pareto Analysis Guide.* Retrieved from: https://www.juran.com/blog/a-guide-to-the-pareto-principle-80-20-rule-pareto-analysis/

importantly, you want to know with certainty (3) why they can be expected to remain your customer into the future.

Imagine if your sales manager or CEO asked you those three questions about each of your key customers. If you are unable to provide a knowledgeable and factual response for each key customer, then you have some work to do! Go and ask. Go and learn. You need to satisfy yourself (with facts, not opinion or "gut" feeling) that you have every right to be confident that your key customers will remain loyal and productive into the foreseeable future.

Understanding your key customer's past, present, and future needs and goals is essential. Having confidence your key customers will remain your customer into the future means you understand how your product(s), service, and relationships will uniquely continue to meet their needs. It implies your understanding of their business is deeply insightful and the relationships you have are strong and secure.

Key Customers Rapport and Relationships

Although you may enjoy the company of your customers, and vice-versa, a business relationship is very different than a personal relationship. Customer relationships are established and strengthened when you understand your customer's needs and goals and especially when you help them meet their needs and accomplish their goals.

Business professionals have corporate goals and initiatives they are responsible to achieve. Business professionals also have personal aspirations for career performance and advancement. When you help your customers achieve their professional goals, and when you are a pleasure to work with, you are well on your way to a solid business relationship.

Know the Decision Makers and Decision Influencers

The relationships you establish with key customers should extend as broadly within the customer's organization as is possible. Whoever is involved with your product either as a decision-maker, a decision influencer, end-user, or purchasing agent should be a person you establish and build a relationship with. A wise man once told me "Anyone in the (customer) building can either help you or hurt you. Be sure you get to know everyone…"

Emphasis should always be placed on building and maintaining relationships with decision-makers and decision influencers. Just as they influence and decide on the purchase of your product, they do the same for potential competing products. Strong rapport and relationship provide you more ready access to the important people and free-flowing exchange of information. Maintain communication so that you always know what your key customer's top priorities are. Ensure that to the extent possible, you help them accomplish their goals and priorities as a trusted resource and business partner.

Business Acumen and Your Key Customer

Anticipating and predicting behaviors accurately is rooted in a deep understanding of what drives your customer's decisions. The obvious common theme is knowing what motivates them currently and what will be motivating them in the future. Such knowledge is a core component of business acumen.

Your business acumen plays a vital role in your ability to anticipate and predict customer behaviors. That is, how well you understand their business as a business along with the associated opportunities and challenges they face. Awareness of industry trends is also part of your business acumen.

Consider all information and data and its potential impact on your customer's business. If your customer is being impacted or soon will be impacted by change, know the implications on your business with them. If there is potential for negative impact, knowing as early as possible allows you to take action to create a solution that enables you to salvage your customer and their business.

On the other hand, positive factors may be in play providing additional opportunities for your customer and therefore your product(s). That is important to know as well and act upon.

Provide Customer Service and Support

The service and support that you provide your key customers are essential to maintaining their business – or not. There is a portion of service and support you personally provide and then there is a portion that your organization provides.

Your responsibility is to know with certainty that your key customers are receiving the level of service and support that is satisfactory to them. That means you know what their requirements and expectations are. To the extent you know your key customer you may be able to anticipate needs that have not yet come into play, but soon will. Be sure you are delivering service and support on a personal level and ensuring that your organization is delivering too.

When problems inevitably arise, handle them promptly and professionally. Problems that are resolved quickly can help to cement your customer's loyalty. Problems that are handled poorly can cause the customer to look for a competitive solution even if the competitive product itself is comparatively inferior. Service and support matter!

Monitor Your Reports

The time to find out a key customer is unhappy, at risk, and then lost is not after their decision to move on has been finalized.

By knowing your key customer's typical purchase and usage patterns you may well identify potential problems early by closely monitoring their purchases as reflected in your sales reports and noting discrepancies. When a customer begins to deviate from previously established purchase patterns there is potentially a problem brewing. This red flag should prompt you to follow up and investigate.

Customers often decrease their purchases when a problem arises, or there is product performance dissatisfaction. If your customer is contemplating moving to a competitive product, they may be purchasing it temporarily or performing a product trial. Did you realize each month of business is 8% of the annual total? That is a lot of business to lose if a key customer is trialing a competitive product. Either way, they have a decreased need to purchase your product and that will show in your sales reports.

Get in, ask questions, and know what is impacting your key customer!

"Why Do You Use This Product?"

What if your competitor asked one of your key customers this question? How would they respond? Think about how you would respond to this question if someone asked you why you use a certain product.

If you had very specific reasons for using a product because that product provided exactly what you needed, then you would likely provide a detailed and enthusiastic response. You would be happy with your purchase, and you would respond accordingly.

On the other hand, if you were ambivalent toward the product, then your response might be very different. If you had to stop and think "yes, why am I using this?" then you might be very open to at least considering an alternative product.

That is the same for your customers. If they were asked this question and if they did not have a well-formed, ready response to that question then they could be at risk.

Be sure that your key customers are happy and satisfied with your product, your company, and you as a resource and business partner. By doing so you provide them reasons to have a ready and positive response.

Application: Identifying, Protecting, and Retaining Customers

Below are the factors involved in identifying, protecting, and retaining current customers. Check any that require your attention, confirmation, or further action. Those factors that are checked represent a risk in your ability to retain one or more key customers.

Factors:

- Key customers have been identified and prioritized for retention.
    - Key customers: are those customers who collectively generate 60% of the territory revenue. The priority is to protect those key customers and ensure they continue to produce revenue in your territory. The secondary priority for key customers is to grow their business.
- I have a full understanding of why my key customers became customers *initially*, why they are customers *currently* – and why they can be expected to remain my customers in the *future*.
- I have a good rapport and strong business relationships within my key customer accounts.
- I know the decision makers and decision influencers.
- I understand my key customer's goals, initiatives, and motivations and how they may impact my business in their account.
- The customer service and support I provide is sufficient to retain my key customer's business.
- I closely monitor key customer purchase patterns and I know their business status.
- My key customers always have a ready response if competitor asks why they use my product.
- Other____

In this exercise, you will identify your key customers and then create your strategic plan to retain them. If you have a sales report available that provides the information below, please use that for reference. If you don't have ready access to such a report then use the template provided to organize your key customers.

Identify your Key Customers:
***Place an asterisk beside the name of any key customers that are at risk of being lost or under threat from competitors.**
****Place two asterisks beside the name of any key customers that have been lost within the past year.**

Name:	Annual Sales:	Factors:

Total Key Customer Sales $\$$________________

Total Key Customer Sales at risk $\$$________________

Total Key Customer Sales Lost $\$$________________

Using the information above, and the factors from your Self-Assessment create your strategic plan to retain your key customers.

By completing each section, you will systematically create your strategic plan. Be succinct yet thorough so that your strategic plan to retain key customers can be used as a meaningful component of your overall plan to achieve quota.

Notes:

____

____

____

____

____

____

____

____

____

____

____

____

Key Customer Retention <u>Goals:</u> (what I am trying to achieve)

____

____

____

____

Key Customer Retention <u>Objectives:</u> (what I must accomplish to achieve my goals)

____

____

____

____

Key Customer Retention <u>Key Performance Indicators:</u> (how I will measure what I am achieving)

____

____

____

____

Key Customer Retention <u>Data, Reports, and Resources:</u> (information and tools I need)

____

____

____

____

Taking into consideration the factors essential to retaining key customers, and especially those factors I identified that may cause certain key customers to be at risk, my strategy to retain key customers is:

____

____

____

____

____

____

____

____

Taking into consideration key customers I identified as being at risk or under competitive threat, my strategy to minimize or counter the threat and retain those key customers is:

____

____

____

____

____

____

____

____

Tactics – the <u>actions</u> I will take when I implement my key customer retention strategies include:

I will (action):   *by (timeline):*

____

____

____

____

____

____

____

____

Notes:

____

____

____

____

____

____

____

____

____

____

Chapter 5: Grow Sales Revenue by Gaining New Customers

Now that you have your plan in place to secure your key customers and their associated sales revenue, let us focus on identifying your best options for growing your sales revenue.

Speaking in very broad terms, there are **three ways** to grow sales revenue. That is, you can **gain new customers**, **grow current customers,** and you can **leverage pricing strategies.** As you seek to grow sales revenue in your territory and when you consider your specific circumstances, you can determine the role each revenue growth opportunity will play in your overall growth strategy.

Grow Sales Revenue: Gain New Customers

Acquiring new customers is fundamental to growing sales revenue today and provides a strong foundation for long-term sales revenue growth and continued success. When determining how new customers can and should fit into your overall growth strategy several factors must be considered. Among them are factors related to your territory, such as the number of potential new customers that exist within your territory and how many of those potential new customers represent qualified opportunities.

Other factors that impact your ability to cultivate and acquire new customers are related to your professional skills. Those skills include your closing success rate and time efficiencies.

Below are the factors that impact your ability to gain new customers along with guidance to maximize each factor for your benefit.

Potential New Customers in My Territory

How many potential new customers exist within your territory? Are there enough potential new customers that you can focus on them as a promising source of the sales revenue growth you must generate? Will those potential new customers provide enough opportunity, quickly enough to meet your revenue growth objective and enable you to achieve quota? Are the potential new customers accessible to you geographically and contractually? Will you be able to meet with them as needed to cultivate them as a customer?

Targeting For Success

How you select and target potential new customers is crucial to your success. Do you have a defined set of parameters that permit you to focus your efforts on high potential targets? A "shotgun" approach is not efficient nor is it effective. It pays to be selective so you can spend your time efficiently and focus on your most promising targets.

You are familiar with the concept of "copy and paste" when working with documents. A similar concept can be applied in your sales efforts too. Consider your best current customers. What are the characteristics that make them great customers? Why is it that your products align so well with their needs? Fully analyze your best current customers and identify the common threads, those attributes that most facilitate a great vendor/customer relationship. Once you have a deep understanding of your best current customers and the traits you should be targeting, then you can use what you have learned to create a template for selecting your best new customer targets that possess those same criteria. Copy and paste.

Prospecting for New Customers

In addition to using your template guidelines to identify new customer targets, successful prospecting depends on how much time you dedicate to prospecting, and secondly, how effective you are in creating viable new sales opportunities from your prospecting activities.

How much prospecting you need to do is directly related to your pipeline needs. If your pipeline is not sufficient to meet your goals, then you must prospect for additional opportunities until your pipeline is healthy. Also, when you close existing pipeline opportunities you should be prospecting for new customer opportunities to add back into your pipeline so that it remains healthy.

You may receive leads that help with your prospecting efforts. If your organization provides you with leads, be sure to follow up quickly as there is typically a very limited window of opportunity while the customer's interest is high.

Qualified New Customer Opportunities

Regardless of the total number of potential new customers in your territory, the real question is how many of the potential new customers represent or can be cultivated into a qualified opportunity? A qualified new customer opportunity means you have confirmed they have a need you can meet and if they decide to purchase your product, they can do so.

Qualified new customer opportunities are viable opportunities that are part of your pipeline.

Once the new customer opportunity has been qualified you also need to quantify the opportunity. In quantifying the opportunity, you confirm how much revenue the opportunity will contribute once it is closed.

Product Price (X) Expected Product Use = Expected Sales Revenue

Known or Confirmed Expected Sales Revenue = Quantified Sales Opportunity

Quantifying new customer opportunities helps to define the level of priority the opportunity represents. It also provides a yardstick for deciding how much time and effort you should be allocating to closing the opportunity. If a new customer opportunity is well qualified and if it will yield significant new sales revenue when it is closed, then the opportunity should be a top priority for your attention, time, and efforts.

You may be able to quantify the opportunity by determining how much of your product the customer expects to use. If the potential customer is using a competitive product, you can use competitive product use as a benchmark. If you are responding to an RFP, it will contain actual or estimated product usage figures.

If none of those options are available, you may resort to using a proxy measure. To create a proxy measure, find a metric you can use to then estimate product usage, and thus, potential sales revenue.

Closing Success Rate

Your ability to close opportunities successfully is a fundamental selling skill and a decisive factor in your ability to grow sales revenue through new customer acquisition. While no one will close every sales opportunity, you cannot successfully grow sales revenue without being proficient at closing.

Your closing success rate is also known as your closing ratio. The total number of pipeline opportunities divided by the number of pipeline opportunities you successfully close equals your closing ratio.

Your closing ratio will be impacted by how well you have qualified the sales opportunity and how well you have cultivated that opportunity through the sales process to the point of closure. Provided you did a good job of qualifying and developing the opportunity, you should have a high level of confidence that the opportunity will close and close within the projected timeline. In such cases, you should close a very high percentage of your sales opportunities.

If closing new customer opportunities is a struggle for you then that is a clear opportunity for improvement of the selling skills that precede the close and/or your closing skills. There is a more detailed discussion on selling skills later in the book.

Time Factors

All sales processes require a certain amount of time. A highly focused and skilled sales professional can minimize the time required to complete and close a sale when compared to a less skilled counterpart. That is because they are extremely efficient and effective in progressing the sale through the steps of their sales process and ultimately, to closure. Your goal in closing new customers should be to do so quickly and efficiently with minimal time delays within your sales process.

How I am defining "quickly" and "efficiently" is according to what is typical for other skilled sales professionals within your organization and within your industry. If a typical sales process requires two weeks for top performers, then that is what you should use as a benchmark for yourself.

Once the customer says "yes" to your offer, certain logistics must be coordinated and navigated before your organization can receive the new sales revenue and before you see the new sales revenue reflected in your sales reports. Those logistics may include receiving the PO, shipping, and delivering the product to your customer. Training, education, or installation may also be required. For products that are purchased monthly, utilization must begin promptly, or you will not see the ongoing sales.

Know the logistics that impact your product(s) and sales process. Ensure all logistics are taken care of expeditiously so that the sales revenue is captured as timely as possible.

Application: Growing Sales Revenue with New Customers

Below are the factors involved in growing sales revenue by gaining new customers. Check all the factors that can be leveraged or improved to enhance your ability to acquire <u>new customers</u> and <u>grow sales revenue</u>.

Factors:

☐ The number of potential new customers within my territory supports new customers as a sales revenue growth opportunity.

☐ I utilize reports and data to analyze, identify, and target high potential new customers.

☐ Prospecting – I invest sufficient time prospecting.

☐ Prospecting – I consistently generate new customer opportunities.

☐ Quali*fied* new customer opportunities – I consistently qualify new customer opportunities.

    ○ "Qualified" means a confirmed, legitimate opportunity exists.

☐ Quantified new customer opportunities – I consistently quantify the dollar value of new customer opportunities to know how much revenue potential each opportunity represents.

☐ Closing success rate – I close a high percentage of pipeline opportunities.

☐ Time – I minimize the time required to close the sale.

☐ Time – I minimize the time required to receive the PO.

☐ Time – I minimize the time required for the new customer to begin product utilization – i.e., how soon the new customer begins using my product.

☐ Other____

Using the reports and data available to you, coupled with your territory knowledge, create a target list of high-value new customer targets. Provide your best estimate of the potential revenue each targeted customer can contribute to your sales year.

Name:	Location:	Potential Revenue:

Total New Customer Potential Sales $___________________

Using the new customer target list, and the factors you identified from your Self-Assessment create your strategic plan to grow sales revenue through acquiring new customers.

By completing each section, you will systematically create your strategic plan. Be succinct yet thorough so that your strategic plan to acquire new customers can be used as a meaningful component of your overall plan to achieve quota.

New Customer Sales Revenue Growth <u>Goals:</u> (what I am trying to achieve)

____

____

____

____

____

New Customer Sales Revenue Growth <u>Objectives</u>: (what I must accomplish to achieve my goals)

____

____

____

____

____

New Customer Sales Revenue Growth <u>Key Performance Indicators</u>: (how I will measure what I am achieving)

____

____

____

____

____

New Customer Sales Revenue Growth <u>Data, Reports, and Resources</u>: (information and tools I need)

____

____

____

____

____

Taking into consideration the factors essential to growing revenue through new customers, especially the factors that impact me most, my strategy to acquire new customers is:

____

____

____

____

____

____

____

____

Tactics – the <u>actions</u> I will take when I implement new customer acquisition and growth strategies include:

I will (action):   *by (timeline):*

____

____

____

____

____

____

____

____

Chapter 6: Grow Sales Revenue with Current Customers

Current customers often represent excellent growth opportunities. They are already familiar with you, and you with them. They have experienced the benefits from your products and the level of service you provide, so a positive impression has been created.

Over the time they have been your customer you have had the opportunity to establish deeper relationships with decision-makers and decision influencers and to know their business more thoroughly.

Since they already do business with you, the logistics associated with purchasing and receiving your products are well established.

For all these reasons, generating additional sales revenue growth with current customers can prove to be faster and easier than cultivating new customers.

Two Ways to Gain Additional Business from Current Customers

The first way to increase sales revenue with current customers is to increase their utilization of the products/services they already use. Have you noticed that your very best customers use a much larger quantity of product compared to other customers, even though both customers are very similar in profile otherwise?

It is important to understand why such a disparity exists, and what can you do to help customers maximize their utilization of your product. Occasionally there are legitimate reasons why a particular customer's volume of business lags when compared to other similar customers. More often, though, a growth opportunity can be cultivated if you invest the time and effort to do so. Be purposeful in managing your customers so that you can help them maximize their potential.

The second way to grow sales revenue with current customers is to sell them additional products and services from your product portfolio. Examples include selling current customers a broader product mix, line extensions, etc.

If the portfolio of products you sell is large you will likely find several of your current customers, even some of your best customers, only use a single product or at most, a very small selection of your products. For the reasons previously mentioned, these customers deserve your attention as potential growth targets.

The factors that impact your ability to effectively grow sales revenue with existing customers are virtually the same as the factors for cultivating new customers, so I won't repeat what was said previously.

What I will say is that remaining vigilant and aggressive minded in seeking growth opportunities is the most important attitude in those who successfully grow sales revenue with existing customers. Far too often a "don't rock the boat" mentality or an "I don't want to pressure my friends" attitude hinders the pursuit of growth opportunities. Ensure that you maintain the right outlook, which is to recognize, create, cultivate, and close new growth opportunities with your existing customers.

Application: Growing Sales Revenue with Existing Customers

Below are the factors involved in growing sales revenue with existing customers. Check all the factors that you can leverage or improve to enhance your ability to grow sales revenue with current customers.

Factors:

☐ I am vigilant and aggressive minded in seeking new growth opportunities with existing customers.

☐ The number of existing customers with growth potential within my territory supports existing customers as a sales revenue growth opportunity.

☐ I utilize reports and data to analyze, identify, and target high potential existing customers.

☐ Prospecting – I invest sufficient time prospecting growth opportunities with existing customers.

☐ Prospecting – I consistently generate new growth opportunities with existing customers.

☐ Quali*fied* existing customer growth opportunities – I consistently qualify new growth opportunities ("Qualified" means a confirmed, legitimate opportunity exists).

☐ Quantified growth opportunities with existing customers – I consistently quantify the dollar value of new opportunities to know how much revenue potential each opportunity represents.

☐ Closing success rate – I close a high percentage of pipeline opportunities.

☐ Time – I minimize the time required to close the sale.

☐ Time – I minimize the time required to receive the PO.

☐ Time – I minimize the time required for my customer to begin new product utilization – i.e., how soon the customer begins using the additional product(s).

☐ Other____

Identify Current Customer Growth Targets:

Name:	Location:	Potential Revenue:

Total Current Customer Growth Opportunities Potential Sales $__________________

Notes:

____

____

____

____

____

____

Current Customer Sales Revenue Growth <u>Goals:</u> (what I am trying to achieve)

____

____

____

____

Current Customer Sales Revenue Growth <u>Objectives</u>: (what I must accomplish to achieve my goals)

____

____

____

____

____

Current Customer Sales Revenue Growth <u>Key Performance Indicators</u>: (how I will measure what I am achieving)

____

____

____

____

____

Current Customer Sales Revenue Growth <u>Data, Reports, and Resources</u>: (information and tools I need)

____

____

____

____

____

Taking into consideration the factors essential to growing revenue with current customers, especially the factors that impact me most, my strategy is:

____

____

____

____

____

____

____

____

Tactics – the <u>actions</u> I will take when I implement my current customer growth strategies include:

I will (action):   *by (timeline):*

____

____

____

____

____

____

____

____

Chapter 7: Grow Sales Revenue with Pricing Strategies

Pricing strategies are the third option for sales revenue growth. Pricing strategies can apply to new and existing customers. Pricing strategies may include:

- Raising the price of your product(s) and/or service(s).
- Optimizing the product mix that you sell by prioritizing more expensive and/or more profitable products.
- Using price incentives to drive greater product volume.

Raise Prices

Raising prices will immediately increase sales revenue but there are a few caveats to consider. The first caveat is that you must have the authority to raise prices. Provided it is within your ability to do then you must determine if the strategy of raising prices is one you wish to implement. Let us examine the pros and cons of raising prices.

You may or may not lose existing customers and potential customers. The key question is whether your current customers and potential customers will tolerate the price increase, or will they look to other suppliers instead?

It is possible that if you raise prices some customers will tolerate the increased prices while others will leave. When there is likely to be a mixed response, you must consider the volume of business can you expect to retain versus what will you lose. If the impact is a net positive there is a rationale to move forward with the price increase.

Depending on the nature of your business, you may enter contracts with customers. If this is the case, then you will likely be contractually bound to a pricing structure for a specified period. During the contracted period, you will not be able to raise prices unless it is provided for within the contract and then, only according to the parameters outlined in the contract. You may also encounter difficulty in renewing the contract when the time comes.

Optimize Product Mix

Some products in your portfolio are likely to be more profitable than others. Whenever possible, prioritize selling products that drive the greatest overall dollar volume and the greatest profitability. By doing so you maximize the overall value each customer contributes to your territory's revenue.

Of course, the first consideration is that the product you sell is the one most appropriate to meet the customer's needs. When products have been updated with a newer and more advanced version of the product the newest versions are typically more expensive than previous versions. Such product advancements represent excellent opportunities to revisit customers who use the older version so you can offer them the most advanced product. There is typically a greater performance benefit for your customers as well. You can benefit both parties by selling the more expensive, more profitable product that performs better and more completely meets their needs.

Incentives: Discounts, Specials, and Promotions

Discounts, specials, and promotions are versions of price incentives offered in exchange for commitment and/or volume. Incentives may be used to entice a new customer or to retain an existing customer. Pricing incentives can be offered to incentivize increased product volumes or close a sale within specific timelines. Whatever the case and desired effect, such incentives can be very popular and effective.

Caution should be taken when pricing incentives become a crutch for sales professionals lacking in closing skills. When you believe or act as if you cannot close the sale without offering price incentives that should raise a red flag that warrants further examination. Strategically offering incentives can be good; using incentives as a band-aid or a routine closing strategy is not.

Selling on price is as old as the profession of selling itself. All sales professionals know that selling on price results in the lowest form of buyer commitment. Selling on price puts the seller at constant risk of losing the next sale to the next guy willing to offer a better price. Selling on price signals to buyers that the product offers minimal value within its market and provides no real advantages compared to its competition.

The way to avoid selling on price is to know your customer's needs, the market in which your product competes, and the product's direct competition. Such knowledge is part of your business acumen. By knowing what each product has to offer and the typical pricing within the market you can make informed strategic pricing decisions. Your product's ability to provide value to your customer and compete successfully against competitive products should dictate pricing, not uncertainties, lack of knowledge, or selling skill deficiencies.

Another caution when offering incentives is the potential to train customers not to buy your product unless and until you provide a "deal." Customers catch on to cyclical or frequent discount patterns and will soon learn to only purchase your product when pricing is discounted, thus minimizing profitability and dollar volume. Don't allow yourself to get into such discounting patterns.

If you typically enter contracts with customers, you need to carefully consider when and how to use pricing incentives. If you set forth pricing in your contract and then offer discounts and incentives unexpectedly within the contract period, the customer may interpret those actions to indicate that your contracted pricing was too high to begin with. When the next contracting cycle comes around, they will be driving hard to get everyday pricing that is in line with the discounts you offered. That is if they don't begin to pressure you before the current contract expires.

The way to avoid that situation is to build into your contract the stipulation that periodic incentives may be offered, or incentives may be offered under specific circumstances. Be sure that you're looking ahead to future contracts and understanding the implications of today's actions on tomorrow's contract. By doing so you will ensure long-term success and not place yourself in a compromised position today, or in the future.

The Pricing Incentive Litmus Test

There are many positive reasons for using pricing incentives. Whatever pricing incentives you select for your sales revenue growth strategy, the outcome must be net revenue growth. Growing sales revenue requires that the pricing incentives you utilize yield net positive results.

If you discount or incentivize to the point that the net result is neutral or even negative, then why do it? Don't lose or give away sales dollars simply to make a deal or get a close.

Application: Grow Sales Revenue with Pricing Strategies

Factors to consider when seeking to grow sales revenue with pricing strategies are listed below. Check all factors that apply to you and your ability to grow sales revenue using pricing strategies.

Factors:

- ☐ Authority – do I have the authority and ability to change pricing?
- ☐ I use pricing incentives as a crutch or band-aid for deficient selling skills or business acumen.
- ☐ Market conditions – will customers tolerate price increases and still use my product/service?
- ☐ I prioritize an optimal product mix where dollar volume and profitability are maximized.
- ☐ Competition – will my competition steal my business if I raise prices?
- ☐ Contractual obligations – I have contracts in place that lock pricing for specified periods.
- ☐ Will I train customers <u>only</u> to buy when incentives are offered?
- ☐ Will I be tempted to overutilize incentives and thereby lose sales dollars unnecessarily?
- ☐ Other____

Notes:

____

____

____

____

____

____

____

____

____

Identify Pricing Targets:

Name:	Annual Sales Gain:	Factors:

Total Potential Sales Increase via Pricing $______________________

Pricing Growth <u>Goals:</u> (what I am trying to achieve)

____

____

____

____

____

Pricing Growth <u>Objectives</u>: (what I must accomplish to achieve my goals)

____

____

____

____

____

Pricing Growth <u>Key Performance Indicators</u>: (how I will measure what I am achieving)

____

____

____

____

____

Pricing Growth <u>Data, Reports, and Resources</u>: (information and tools I need)

____

____

____

____

____

Taking into consideration the factors essential to generating additional sales revenue via pricing strategies, and those factors that impact me most, my strategy to grow sales revenue with pricing is:

____

____

____

____

____

____

____

____

Tactics – the <u>actions</u> I will take when I implement my pricing growth strategies include:

I will (action):   *by (timeline):*

____

____

____

____

____

____

____

____

____

Chapter 8: My Strategic Plan to Achieve Quota

To this point, we have discussed the numerous components and strategies that go into making your quota. Those components included the quota formula and the various sales revenue dynamics you must interpret and account for. Also included were the concepts of net growth objective and goal setting for monthly and annual new sales revenue. We defined what a healthy pipeline is and analyzed your current pipeline's health status. The importance of identifying and retaining key customers was highlighted. In addition, we examined three strategies to grow sales revenue and you identified those that represent your best growth opportunities.

As each topic was discussed you input data and you created goals and strategies. Now is the time to review the notes you made along with the individual goals and strategies you have created so you can integrate them into one cohesive strategic plan to attain your quota.

At the end of the strategic plan form below, there is a line for you to indicate the person who will serve as your accountability partner. Why? And who should that person be?

The reason an accountability partner is important is that Psychology professor Dr. Gail Matthews found goal achievement in the workplace was influenced by three key actions: **"writing goals, committing to goal-directed actions, and lastly, creating accountability for those actions."** By doing these three things, study participants were able to escalate their success rate up to 76%![7]

As you have been completing the applications at the end of each section, you have been systematically creating the foundation of your strategic plan. You have written your goals along with the objectives, strategies, and tactics. To add the third component of successful goal

---

[7] Gardner, S. & Albee, D. (2015). *Study focuses on strategies for achieving goals, resolutions*. Dominican University of California. Retrieved from: https://scholar.dominican.edu/news-releases/266

achievement, accountability, you will identify your accountability partner, who will help you to stay focused and on track.

Given the responsibility and importance of your accountability partner, my suggestion is that your sales leader should be your accountability partner. If for some reason that is not the best person for you, then identify someone who will be the best accountability partner for you.

When you complete your strategic plan, review it with your accountability partner. Schedule update meetings to review your progress. The key is frequent, open, and honest communication so that you stay true to your plan and execute it in a disciplined manner.

You may need to update your plan along the way, and that is perfectly okay to do. But stay focused on your goals and be sure that you keep your actions aligned to your goals. Work with your accountability partner to ensure you perform at your very best and achieve your quota!

Application: Strategic Plan Template

Quota Attainment <u>Goal(s):</u> (what I am trying to achieve)

____

____

____

____

Quota Attainment <u>Objectives</u>: (what I must accomplish to achieve my quota goals)

____

____

____

____

Quota Attainment <u>Key Performance Indicators (KPIs)</u>: (how I will measure what I am achieving)

____

____

____

____

Quota Attainment <u>Data, Reports, and Resources</u>: (information and tools I need)

____

____

____

____

Taking into consideration the factors essential to attaining quota, and especially sales revenue dynamics that impact my territory and my best potential for sales revenue growth, my strategy to attain quota is:

____

____

____

____

____

____

____

Taking into consideration any total market decline or negative market share change as well as any known negative carry forward from lost customers, my strategy to overcome "negative headwinds" is:

____

____

____

____

____

____

____

Tactics – the <u>actions</u> I will take when I implement my quota attainment strategies include:

I will (action):   *by (timeline):*

____

____

____

____

____

____

____

____

I will create an accountability process with:

____

Notes:

____

____

____

____

____

____

____

SECTION 2: HOW TO GET BACK ON TRACK WHEN THERE'S A GAP

I love the optimism that is deeply embedded in most sales professionals. The can-do attitude and glass half full mentality is a winning combination, except when it prevents the reality of the situation from registering as the threat it truly represents.

I once knew a sales professional who got behind his quota early in the year. We spoke frequently about his plan for course correction. He assured me that he was fully confident that he would hit his goal by yearend.

As fall approached, he was still behind his quota and little progress had been made in closing the gap. We reviewed his data together over a cup of coffee. We looked at the gap in his year-to-date sales compared to his quota. We then combed through his pipeline and added the expected new sales revenue that would occur by yearend. The math simply did not add up. Though we had reviewed this information many times before, this was the first time something clicked for him. As he stared at the computer screen, he realized that his pipeline would not get him to quota, even if he closed everything in it exactly when he projected. Since he had not been prospecting as aggressively as he should have, there was nothing of substance that he could add to his pipeline to further overcome the gap.

He stared at that laptop for several minutes as it all soaked in. He looked up at me and said "Kevin, I'm not going to make my quota this year."

According to various sources, between 46% and 57% of sales professionals perform under their quota.[8][9][10] If your sales results are not meeting your sales goals, when should action be taken? What should your next steps be to fully understand the root cause(s), modify your strategic plan, and take the actions that allow you to rectify the situation?

Section Goals

- **Know when and how to course correct.**
- **Understand why you are underperforming, including root cause analysis.**
- **Craft your strategic plan to course correct and get yourself back on track.**

---

[8] CSO Insights: The Research Division of Miller Heiman Group. (2018). *Selling in the Age of Ceaseless Change: The 2018-2019 Sales Performance Report.* Retrieved from: http://online.pubhtml5.com/bwdb/ldyb/ldyb.pdf

[9] Hyken, S. (2018, Sept. 2). *57% of Sales Reps Missed Their Quotas Last Year*. Forbes. Retrieved from: https://www.forbes.com/sites/shephyken/2018/09/02/77-of-sales-reps-missed-their-quotas-last-year/?sh=c98f89d52e4b

[10] Martin, S.W. (2013, Dec. 9). *The Twelve Sales Metrics that Matter Most*. Harvard Business Review. Retrieved from: https://hbr.org/2013/12/new-insight-into-key-sales-metrics

Chapter 9: When and How to Take Corrective Action

Any time your sales results are not meeting your sales goals it should get your full attention. Many organizations assign quarterly sales expectations, along with your quota for the full year. Each month's performance is vital to your quarterly success. You cannot afford to fall behind for more than a month, or your quarterly goal attainment will be at risk. Each month your sales goals are not met increases the risk of missing your annual quota, as well.

Don't fall into the trap of thinking that action is not needed because the year is young, and you will eventually (somehow) get yourself back on track. Many sales professionals who fail to act early find that although their sales year is far from over, they get too far behind quota and run out of time for corrective measures to be fully effective. By the time it becomes evident to them that they will not be able to meet their annual quota their fate for the year is sealed. The reality is that time is only on your side when you take corrective action quickly. As each month goes by time is more and more your enemy.

Course correction begins by ascertaining why you are behind your goals. Start your analysis by scrutinizing your sales reports and data. You need to discover the root cause of your underperformance and why it is occurring. Is there some anomaly that is causing what you know to be a temporary underperformance? If you do nothing, are you confident that your sales results will change so that you will achieve your quota?

If you cannot definitively answer "yes" to the last question, then you need to take corrective action. And the sooner that you take corrective action, the better your chances of having enough time to make up for insufficient sales and achieve your quota by year's-end. You must have a strong sense of urgency and a willingness to take action.

Communicate with Your Manager

Any time you are not achieving your year-to-date (YTD) sales goals I strongly recommend that you communicate with your sales manager. When I suggest that you communicate with your sales manager, what I mean is that you take the lead and initiate the conversation. Discuss your YTD performance and what you are doing to correct it.

As a former sales leader, I can assure you that your manager is acutely aware you are behind quota. What they want to know from you is that you are being proactive, that you have a plan, and that you are acting on it!

Communicate the root cause and the steps you are taking to rectify the situation. By being proactive, you demonstrate your willingness to take responsibility for your performance, and that you are determined to raise your performance and meet your goals. You also demonstrate that you can analyze and problem-solve. Review your plan with them. Your sales leader will likely be able to provide additional insights, support, and resources to help you move forward.

Recognize Sales Trends Early

The reason to recognize sales trends early and be proactive is that time is only on your side early in the year. As the year progresses, time becomes your enemy. By identifying, resolving, and overcoming the root cause of your challenge early in the year you have time to recover and achieve your goals. However, the same turnaround will not allow you to achieve your annual quota if it comes too late in the year. Instead, you will simply run out of time.

To analyze your sales trends, thoroughly review your sales reports and territory data, as well as any other data resources that will be helpful to you in your analysis. Be sure to consider all that you have learned from your daily activities and customer conversations as well. The goal is to get a complete and accurate picture of the underlying causes, effects, and implications of your current sales results. Go through the information carefully, and without bias or preconceptions that may otherwise cause you to miss important insights.

Carefully analyze your sales trends and associated reports every month. Careful analysis means reviewing all data and sales trends to recognize what is happening (good or bad) and understanding why so that you can anticipate and forecast what will occur in the coming months and respond accordingly.

Data to review includes:

- PY monthly and total sales (baseline sales).
- PY monthly sales by customer.
- PY monthly sales by product.
- YTD total sales results by month.
- YTD monthly sales by customer.
- YTD monthly sales by product.
- All relevant customer insights and feedback.
- All relevant organizational insights and feedback.
- Industry news.

You may have additional data available to you that is useful in your analysis. Review and analyze all relevant data.

Implied Quarterly and Annual Results

The analysis includes twelve-month, three-month, and one-month rates of change. How do your most recent month and most recent three months compare? Is the trend positive, negative, or flat? How do the most recent three months compare to the most recent twelve months? Is the trend positive, negative, or flat? If the change is positive or negative, is the rate of change accelerating or decelerating? And, what do the trends imply relative to your net growth objective and quota?

Typical analysis may include:

- What are YTD results vs YTD quota?
    - Examine the quota deficit.
- What is your YTD quota deficit?
- Is this an anomaly? Why or why not?
- What is your average monthly quota deficit?
- Are you falling increasingly behind your annual quota each month, or are you getting closer to quota each month? Why?
- What are the implications of the sales trend continuing as-is for the rest of the year?
    - Review the three-month run rate (3-Mo RR).
- Formula: Month 1 sales + Month 2 sales + Month 3 sales = $X. $X/3 = 3-Mo RR.
- Refer to your most recent three months.
- What is your projected performance versus quota using your Three-Month Run Rate?
    - Analyze the three-month rate of growth or decline.
- What is the most recent three-month sales trend versus prior three-month and prior twelve-months sales?
- When did the sales trend change? Why?
- What customers and products are part of the downturn or lagging performance? Again, why is this?
- Using these numbers, project your performance versus your goals.
- Is the projection an anomaly? Why or why not?
- How do your most recent month's sales compare to your 3-month run rate? What are the implications if the remainder of the year's monthly sales matched your most recent month?

Let's be honest here, no salesperson likes to spend inordinate amounts of time digging through reports and doing the math. It is especially discouraging when the numbers are negative. In fact, it can be downright depressing! However, the answers you need are in your reports, so you must do the analysis and you must persist until you find the root cause. Only then can you identify how you can correct the situation.

As an aside, if you aspire to a management role then you need to be very effective in analyzing reports because that is a critical and routine element of the job. Even if you do not aspire to such a position, by becoming skillful in analyzing your data and reports you will greatly increase your effectiveness in your current role.

Root Cause Analysis

A root cause analysis might be described as a quest for what, why, who, how much, and for how long? The goal is to identify the root cause(s) that led to everything else and to fully understand it. Some root cause analysis processes require you to answer "why" as many as seven times to get to the most granular detail possible.

The data and reports available to you should reveal much of the detail you need. Identify all the accounts that are underperforming YTD expectations or, are negative when compared to the same period in the previous year.

Answer the questions above. Once you have answered "what" and "who" dig deeper to discover why, why, why... Why are the accounts lost? If they are not lost, but purchasing less product than anticipated, why is that? Dig until you know why.

How much and for how long? Quantify your data. Know the degree of impact each negative account is contributing to your results.

- Which of your customers are down vs. prior year sales? Why?
- Which of your products are down vs. prior year sales? Why?
- What trends are occurring in your territory that negatively impacts your sales? Why?
- What industry trends are occurring that are negatively impacting your sales? Why?
- Are competitors taking customers from you? Or are they impacting your ability to close enough new opportunities? If so, why is this occurring?
- **"Why" is the key question. Continue asking "why" until you get to the root cause(s).**

Notes:

Application: Customer Trends

In order of magnitude, what account(s) is/are down and why? Complete the chart below:

Top Accounts w/ Losses:	YTD Losses:	Why Account is Underperforming or Lost:

Implications of these trends for the rest of the sales year:

____

____

____

____

____

____

____

Application: Product Trends

What product(s) is/are down and why? Complete the chart below:

Top 5 Products w/ Losses:	YTD Losses:	Why Product is Underperforming:

What are the product trends implications for the rest of the sales year?

____

____

____

____

____

____

____

____

____

____

____

The other important resource you have for root cause analysis is… yourself. You know your territory, your customers, your strategic plan to achieve quota, your pipeline, and the YTD new business that you've generated. You also know your attitude and effort. Any, or all of these may be contributing factors to your underperformance.

Now is the time to be very honest with yourself and to be specific so that you can create an effective plan to remedy your performance.

Notes:

____

____

____

____

____

____

____

____

____

____

____

____

Application: Other Negative Impacts

In addition to the factors that you previously reviewed and analyzed, what else is negatively impacting your sales results? Some common factors are identified below. Check all that apply:

☐ Time Management and Territory Management:

    ☐ Too little time spent with priority accounts (target or existing).

    ☐ Too much time spent with non-priority accounts.

    ☐ Not enough face-to-face selling time.

    ☐ Inefficient routing.

☐ Pipeline Management:

    ☐ Insufficient qualified new opportunities were created and added to the pipeline.

    ☐ Cultivation of opportunities and progressing them, timely and efficiently, through the sales process to closure.

    ☐ Insufficient number and/or size of closes.

    ☐ Insufficient total pipeline.

☐ Rapport and Relationships:

    ☐ Insufficient relationships with decision-makers and decision-influencers.

    ☐ Relationships are not deep enough and/or wide enough in key accounts.

    ☐ Not consistently becoming a trusted advisor and resource.

☐ Selling Skills:

    ☐ Lacking a consistent, repeatable sales process.

    ☐ Inconsistent probing skills or probing strategy.

    ☐ Product presentations/product demonstrations fail to consistently produce positive outcomes.

    ☐ Insufficiently persuasive.

    ☐ Inability to read buying signals/non-verbal communication.

    ☐ Inconsistent in overcoming objections.

- ☐ Inconsistent closing skills/gaining commitment/generating action.
☐ Business Acumen:
  - ☐ Need to better understand your own business operations, procedures, and profit drivers.
  - ☐ Need to better understand your customer's business model.
  - ☐ Need to become a solutions provider instead of simply transactional.
  - ☐ Need to better create value internally/externally.
  - ☐ Need to better create "win/win" scenarios.
☐ Attitude:
  - ☐ Inconsistent "hunter" mentality to aggressively create and cultivate new business.
  - ☐ Lacking sufficient determination.
  - ☐ Pessimistic outlook.
  - ☐ Distracted by F.U.D. (Fear, Uncertainty, and Doubt).
  - ☐ Lacking sufficient persistence.
  - ☐ Lacking sufficient resilience.
  - ☐ Needs more resourcefulness and creativity.
  - ☐ Other:____

____

Notes:

____

____

____

____

____

____

____

For each checked box, describe how the factor is affecting your ability to be successful. Specify the changes that are needed to improve in that area:

Factor   **Effect on Results**   **Changes Needed**

____

____

____

____

____

____

____

____

____

____

____

____

____

____

____

____

***Skills and attitude are discussed in more detail later. You will be able to create specific goals, objectives, strategies, and tactics to target and build proficiencies.**

Chapter 10: Determine the Sales Revenue Needed to Fill the Gap

Now that you have a more detailed understanding of your YTD results including root causes, and insight as to why those challenges are occurring, you need to create a strategic plan that will enable you to course correct and reach your goals.

To begin, determine the monthly sales revenue required for you to overcome your YTD quota deficit and get back on track to achieve your quota. Once that number is identified, continue to review, and revise your monthly sales revenue goals each month throughout the year. Doing this will ensure you have accurate monthly sales revenue goals that when achieved, lead to you meeting your year-end quota.

Non-Recurring Sales – Revised Monthly New Sales Revenue Goal Methodology

To create a new monthly revenue goal for products that are sold in a non-recurring fashion, take your remaining quota, and divide it by the number of months remaining in the year.

For example, if your remaining annual quota is $100,000 and you have 7 months left in the year, you would need to sell an average of $14,286 each month to achieve your quota. I.e., $100,000 / 7 = $14,286.

NOTE: Repeat the same calculation each month. In doing so, your monthly revenue goals will be clear, accurate, and always up to date.

Recurring Sales – Revised Monthly New Sales Revenue Goal Methodology

For products with recurring monthly sales, use the Rule of 78s. For convenience, the Rule of 78s Chart is below (Figure 10.1).

Figure 10.1

	Jan	Feb	Mar	Apr	May	Jun	Jul	Aug	Sep	Oct	Nov	Dec	# Periods
Jan	X	X	X	X	X	X	X	X	X	X	X	X	78
Feb		X	X	X	X	X	X	X	X	X	X	X	66
Mar			X	X	X	X	X	X	X	X	X	X	55
Apr				X	X	X	X	X	X	X	X	X	45
May					X	X	X	X	X	X	X	X	36
Jun						X	X	X	X	X	X	X	28
Jul							X	X	X	X	X	X	21
Aug								X	X	X	X	X	15
Sep									X	X	X	X	10
Oct										X	X	X	6
Nov											X	X	3
Dec												X	1

Recall that each "X" represents a purchasing period and as you can see, the number of purchasing periods declines from month to month through the course of the year. The number of periods remaining in the year is listed for each month in the far-right column. To calculate the monthly new sales revenue required to achieve your year-end quota, focus on your **YTD growth objective**. That is, how much revenue growth is still required over YTD sales to achieve quota?

As an example, let us suppose it is April and our remaining growth objective is $191,795. The $191,795 must be generated between April and December. By referring to the Rule of 78s chart above, we can see that only 45 periods remain in the year. Let's do the math:

$191,795 / 45 = **$4,262**.

The Rule of 78s can be used in this way to determine a new monthly close goal at any time during the year. To revise the monthly close goal simply divide the remaining growth objective by the number of periods left in the fiscal year.

One final example: the remaining growth objective YTD is $160,000 as of August. How much will we need to close in new, recurring business each month for the remainder of the year? Referencing the chart, we see that as of August, 15 periods remain in the year. The calculation is: $160,000 / 15 periods = $10,667.

To recap, for products with recurring monthly sales, the Rule of 78s enables you to calculate monthly close goals throughout the year. By doing this, you know exactly what new sales revenue you need to generate each month to hit your year-end quota.

Application: Revised Monthly New Sales Revenue Goal

Non-Recurring Sales:

Quota remaining divided by the number of months remaining in the year = Monthly Close Goal:

$_________________ / # months _________________ = Monthly Close Goal: $_________________

Recurring Sales:

Remaining Net Growth Objective divided by the number of remaining periods in the year = Monthly Close Goal:

$_________________ / # periods _________________ = Monthly Close Goal: $_________________

Notes:

____

____

____

____

____

____

____

____

____

____

____

Chapter 11: Sales Pipeline Review

Now that you have projected the sales revenue growth you need to achieve quota, you will need to determine whether your current pipeline of opportunities is sufficient. Remember that your pipeline has two important metrics: the combined **value** of the opportunities and the **timeline** for closing them.

A **healthy pipeline** contains *realistic, qualified, and quantified* opportunities, with revenue totaling at least 3 to 4 times the sales revenue growth needed to achieve your goals. Additionally, the *timeframe* for closing the opportunities is crucial. You must ensure that the revenue from closes will be generated and captured on your sales reports within a timeframe that allows you to achieve quota. If either of these requirements is not sufficient to meet your goals, then your pipeline must be adjusted accordingly. That is, add additional qualified opportunities until you have 3 to 4 times the sales revenue growth needed to achieve your goals and/or speed the progression of your existing opportunities so that they can close according to your timeline requirements.

Application: Pipeline Review

Fill in the blanks below. In the monthly column provide the total sales revenue you expect to gain from your current pipeline of opportunities. Provide the sum of non-recurring sales and recurring sales. Then, compare the revenue you expect to gain to the revised monthly close goal you previously identified.

Do the same calculations for your annual totals.

Total $ value of Pipeline $\geq$75% Confidence: Monthly   Annual

    Non-Recurring Sales $\$$____________ $\$$____________

    Recurring Sales   + $\$$____________   + $\$$____________

    Expected $ Growth   = $\$$____________   = $\$$____________

    Growth required to achieve quota $\$$____________ $\$$____________

Does your current pipeline provide enough **new sales volume** to sufficiently meet your monthly and annual growth objectives? Will your opportunities **close soon enough,** within the current month and the sales year, to achieve monthly close goals and annual quota? **Yes / No**

____

____

____

____

If not, how will you develop your pipeline so that it provides sufficient revenue on time for you to achieve quota?

____

____

____

____

____

IMPORTANT! Repeat this application exercise <u>each month</u> until your YTD sales results are meeting your YTD quota.

NOTE: if you have multiple products and/or services each with its own quotas, you will need to do this same pipeline review for each. Pipeline templates are available in the appendix.

Notes:

____

____

____

____

____

____

____

____

____

Chapter 12: Create Your Course Correction Strategic Plan

Let's recap. To effectively course correct you must first have a detailed understanding of why your sales performance is underperforming your YTD Quota. To that end, the steps you have taken so far include:

- A root cause analysis including:
    - Data analysis of available reports.
    - Customer performance.
    - Product performance.
    - Personal performance.
- Calculated sales revenue required to overcome the YTD quota deficit.
- Calculated new sales revenue monthly goals.
- Performed a pipeline 'health confirmation'.

You are now ready to create a plan of action to accomplish your mid-year course correction to get yourself back on track to achieve your quota.

Application: Mid-Year Course Correction Strategy

To create your strategic plan for course correction, review the information you have compiled and using what you have learned, complete the following template.

Course Correction <u>Goals:</u> (what I am trying to achieve)

____

____

____

____

Course Correction <u>Objectives</u>: (what I must accomplish to achieve my goals)

____

____

____

____

Course Correction <u>Key Performance Indicators</u>: (how I will measure what I am achieving)

____

____

____

Course Correction <u>Data, Reports, and Resources</u>: (information and tools I need)

____

____

____

____

Taking into consideration the factors essential to correcting my YTD quota attainment, and those factors that impact me most, my strategy for mid-year course correction is:

____

____

____

____

____

____

____

____

Tactics – the <u>actions</u> I will take when I implement my mid-year course correction strategies include:

I will (action):   *by (timeline):*

____

____

____

____

____

____

____

____

____

____

Now that you have created your plan it would be wise to review it with your sales manager. Discuss the data analysis you performed, the root cause(s), and your plan to course correct. Be sure that you have your manager's buy-in and support.

The next step is to go and execute your plan. Follow your strategies and execute your tactics with urgency and diligence. Continue to gather information, communicate frequently and openly with your sales leader.

Notes:

____

____

____

____

____

____

____

____

____

____

____

____

Key Performance Indicators

In your strategic plan, you listed key performance indicators (KPIs). KPIs are there to confirm that you are on track to achieve your goal. Your KPIs should include your revised monthly new sales revenue goal and results. KPIs should also include the YTD quota and YTD results. List as a KPI what your pipeline goals are monthly along with your pipeline data to include new pipeline additions, expected closes for the coming month, and actual closes that occurred. There may be other KPIs that are important to you, especially if you have other strategic initiatives that you are responsible for delivering.

This may sound like a lot of administrative tasks but there is not a better or more effective way to objectively confirm that your plan is working. If you find that your plan is not getting you to your goal, then review the data. Also review your objectives, strategies, and tactics. Where necessary, make the updates to your plan.

Attitude

When sales performance is not where you want it is easy to get discouraged. Fight any urges to get down on yourself or frustrated. Focus on your plan and execute your plan. Be disciplined and act with urgency.

Eliminate sources of negativity so that you don't become distracted. Control what you can control, which is your plan, priorities, time management, and your actions. Stay relentlessly resilient! That is, any time that you feel pressured or affected by F.U.D. (fear, uncertainty, and doubt), make a conscious decision to ignore the unproductive distractions. Be determined because you can do this and when you accomplish your goal everything you did will have been worth the effort.

Keys to Rectifying the Situation

- Frequent, open, and ongoing communication with your sales manager.
- Take corrective action quickly – don't assume results will get better with no intervention!
- Recognize sales trends and challenges as early in the fiscal year as possible.

- Understand implied quarterly and annual results.

- Thoroughly analyze root causes: what, why, how much, and for how long?

- Determine the sales revenue needed to fill the performance gap and achieve quota.

- Confirm your pipeline supports your new monthly and annual goals.

- Create your course correction plan. Review and revise your **G**oals, **O**bjectives, **S**trategies, and **T**actics **(G.O.S.T.).**
    - Explore and select your best options for increasing sales revenue.
    - Create your new sales plan – <u>write out</u> your revised **G.O.S.T.**

- Diligently execute your revised strategy and tactics.

- **K**ey **P**erformance **I**ndicators:
    - Select the KPIs that are critical to your success.
    - Monitor KPIs frequently.
    - Determine if your strategy and tactics are working as planned.
    - Further course correct if needed, as needed.

- Mind your attitude! Be positive, be resilient, and be determined. You can do this!

Performance Improvement Plans

Depending on your YTD performance and overall performance history at your current organization it is possible that you will find yourself being put on a PIP (Performance Improvement Plan) when you are underperforming your assigned quota. If you are issued a PIP, what should you do?

First, recognize the basic steps that have been outlined throughout this book directly apply to how you should approach creating your plan for meeting the goals specified on your PIP. Starting with those goals, follow the G.O.S.T. methodology and create your strategic plan. Be aware of the timelines and KPIs so that you can ensure your strategic plan accounts for all deliverables and timelines stipulated within your PIP.

What are the implications of a PIP? PIPs are created when the organization and/or sales management feel the need to issue an ultimatum. The ultimatum is: either meet the assigned goals by the deadlines identified in the PIP or you will no longer be part of that organization. That may sound harsh, but it is the reality of the situation. Knowing that, you must evaluate your options.

If you want to remain with your organization, you need to have a frank conversation with your manager. A PIP will have certain goals you must achieve. Those goals "should" be reasonable and attainable. When you are speaking with your manager, seek to understand the goals and how they were determined. Those goals may be a real stretch, but they should be realistic and attainable. Review each of them with your manager to confirm you have a full understanding of what you must deliver, and by when. If you feel the goals are not realistic then seek agreement on what can be changed. That is, provided they are willing to do so.

Ask your manager to help you strategize. Be sure to communicate that you value your position, and you will do everything within your power to successfully complete the PIP because you want to retain your job. Update your manager on your progress frequently. Be proactive and communicative because your job depends on it!

The other obvious choice you have is to find another position. Only you can determine if that is your best choice but sometimes a change of scenery and a fresh start is the better option. Even if that is your choice, do not simply move on without deep soul searching and a root cause analysis. If you have professional shortcomings that you do not address you may soon find yourself in another challenging situation. The key is to learn from your challenges and do what is necessary to overcome them.

All of us have areas of strength and other areas that are not as strong. We can all learn, practice, and improve. We can all "work smarter" and perform better. That is the basis for Section 3: Working the Sales Process, where we will explore more effective and more efficient ways to directly impact performance, and thus, quota attainment.

SECTION 3: WORKING THE SALES PROCESS

How many times have you heard the phrase "work smarter, not harder?" That sounds like good advice, but how is it that we can work smarter?

Professional athletes possess skills and abilities that separate them from the rest of us mere mortals. If we were competing against them, they could easily defeat us simply by relying on those skills and abilities. However, to win against other professional athletes with similar skill sets and abilities requires more. Professionals who win against talented competitors do so by practicing and honing their skills to a razor's edge, employing superior gameplans, better strategies, and exceptional execution. Similarly, sales professionals who consistently achieve and outperform their peers and competitors do so by polishing their skills, employing superior game plans, better strategies, and unerring execution.

Superior game plans and better strategies trace their roots back to all the things that were covered earlier, such as understanding territory sales revenue trends, knowing your net sales revenue growth objective, and identifying your best revenue growth opportunities. All those data points, and the other topics we discussed earlier underlie your ability to build an effective strategic plan.

Having constructed your strategic plan, now your attention can turn to how you will best execute it. Executing your strategic plan at your highest level so that you consistently achieve quota and perform at your very best means wisely using your professional skills to maximize efficiency and outcomes. This is the essence of "working smarter" to produce your best results.

Working smarter is the focus for the following topics. We will explore how to maximize your professional skills and the strategies that directly impact your overall effectiveness in growing sales revenue and achieving quota.

The skills and strategies that we will focus on to maximize efficiency and results include:

- Sales process.
- Probing strategy.
- Overcoming objections.
- Gaining commitment.
- Pipeline management.
- Business acumen.
- Increasing the quantity of sales opportunities.
- Increasing qualified sales opportunities.
- Increasing the revenue potential of sales opportunities.
- Reducing time.
- The three pillars of success.
- Product knowledge.
- Coachability and self-management.
- Compete to Win!

Section Goals

- **Maximize sales effectiveness.**
- **Identify effective strategies to work smarter and more efficiently.**

Chapter 13: Sales Process

Sales Process – Defined, refined, and repeatable

Successful people know there are certain ways of doing things that produce optimal results. Have you ever watched a skilled craftsman work? They follow a process - a thoughtfully refined sequence of steps that lead to a finished product. It is their craft, and they approach it as such. Each step in their process has been honed and perfected over time by practice and repetition so that in the end, they consistently produce the outcome they are seeking.

Similarly, top sales professionals have a consistent, repeatable sales process they follow because it works. A good sales process enables them to become better and better; faster and faster at generating sales results. It produces consistent outcomes that meet and exceed goals. Every Sales professional must have a strong sales process to be their most productive.

Defined Steps with Clear Goals – The Goal-Based Selling Process

What steps or stages comprise your sales process? Whether your sales process can be completed in only one meeting or if it requires a series of meetings there are steps or progressive stages that typically occur.

A sales process involves a sequence of steps, with specific goals to be accomplished at each step. An example is the Goal-Based Selling process. You have already been exposed to elements of this sales process throughout this book.

Goal-Based Selling (GBS) is the process of identifying and using goals to guide every facet of what we do as sales professionals. The GBS Sales Process provides a sequential pathway from opportunity identification to ultimately closing the sale and then implementing the product. Your typical sales process may vary slightly but will ultimately follow a similar structure.

GBS Sales Process Step 1

The first step of GBS is opportunity analysis. The goal of GBS Sales Process Step One is to identify and select the best prospective, targeted sales revenue opportunities that will enable you to meet and surpass your quota and any other strategic initiatives you are responsible for.

In this step, you use the reports and other resources available to identify your best and largest growth opportunities. A target list of prospective accounts is created or updated to include the targeted accounts and the targeted product opportunities that, when added together, equal 3-4 times your growth objective or quota as applicable to your specific requirements. Once you have your prospect target list compiled you are ready to proceed to the second step.

GBS Sales Process Step 2

The second step in the GBS Sales Process is the live customer interactions during a meeting or over a series of meetings. The goals of GBS Sales Process Step Two are:

- Qualify and quantify your targeted opportunities – confirm that product conversion opportunities exist within the account and determine the annual value.
- Develop a mutual understanding of customer needs.
- Present and demonstrate your solution. Establish that your solution(s) represent the best choice and yield outcomes in line with customer goals.
- Gain Product Trial / Evaluation (If applicable for your product or solution).

The second step of GBS involves in-person discussions with the targeted customers' Decision Makers and Decision Influencers. During the discussions, you *qualify* and *quantify* each opportunity. That is, you confirm that a valid opportunity exists, along with the sales revenue potential.

If, during those discussions, you find that a targeted opportunity is <u>not</u> a valid target, replace that target with the next best one until you have a robust pipeline of qualified, quantified, and validated opportunities.

The process of qualifying and quantifying new opportunities and adding them to your pipeline is constantly repeated and managed throughout the year so that you can achieve your current year's goals and set yourself up to achieve the following year's goals as well. Proactive opportunity identification, qualification & quantification is essential and an ongoing part of building and maintaining a healthy pipeline.

During this phase, you are discovering and developing customer needs. You use your probing skills and probing strategy to uncover and confirm information that enables you to fully understand your customer's goals, priorities, decision criteria, needs, and wants. By doing so you can position your solution appropriately.

Once you have a complete understanding of customer goals, priorities, decision criteria, needs, and wants, you can then present your product. And you can show them how your solution meets their needs and enables them to improve their outcomes by providing a hands-on product demonstration.

The product presentation and demonstration are pivotal moments in the GBS Sales Process. This is your opportunity to align the presentation of your product to the Decision Maker's and Decision Influencer's previously expressed goals, priorities, decision criteria, needs, and wants. It is your time to prove that your product is the right choice and provides exactly the solution they are seeking.

Allowing your customer to experience your product in action is an essential part of the presentation. An effective demonstration actively involves the customer and engages as many of the five senses as you can involve. The demonstration provides them evidence and establishes how your product yields the desired outcome goals and meets (and exceeds) their needs and wants.

If you have fully understood (and confirmed) their goals, priorities, needs, and wants, and if you have properly positioned your solution and provided an effective product demonstration, you should be able to gain your customer's agreement to move the process forward to the next step.

Depending on the nature of your product and your customer's purchasing process, the next step may be to close the sale. Some customers, though, require the additional step of a product trial. If a product trial is required, that would be GBS Sales Process Step 3.

GBS Sales Process Step 3

The third step in the GBS Sales Process is the customer experiencing the product in the form of a product trial. The goals of GBS Sales Process Step 3 are:

- If required or desirable, conduct a successful product trial during which the prospective customer sees the product yield the desired results that will ultimately lead to product conversion.
- Earn the prospective customer's commitment to purchase the product(s) being trialed.

If a product trial is required, it is essential that you and your customer first mutually agree upon any outcome goals that must be achieved for the trial to be considered a success. Ensure you understand what will constitute a successful trial and that those goals are mutually agreed upon before beginning the product trial. Only once you have a full, complete mutual understanding with your customer regarding the trial goals, how the trial will be conducted, those who will be involved, and the duration of the trial, do you move forward and begin the trial.

Provided the product trial met all mutually agreed upon outcome goals your next step is to close the sale and prepare for the product conversion and implementation. That is GBS Sales Process Step 4.

GBS Sales Process Step 4

The fourth step in the GBS Sales Process is closing and implementing the product or service. The goal of GBS Sales Process Step 4 is to confirm the prospective customer's commitment to purchase the product(s) being trialed i.e., close the sale.

Successfully closing the sale and then implementing the product require careful planning and coordination of any educational or training requirements and the logistical aspects involved in bringing in the new product. Also, consistent follow-up is required in the months immediately following the sale to ensure strong product adoption, utilization, and long-term success.

This overview of the GBS Sales Process as presented provides a general template that you can adapt to your selling scenario and customer purchasing process as needed. When the GBS Sales Process was implemented in organizations I worked with each GBS step was customized to their selling environment and products. Each step contained much more detail as appropriate to their sales environment. The detail for each step included the goals for each step, strategies, tactics, and a list of resources.

Aligned to Your Customer's Purchasing Process

Just as you have your sales process, many customers have a specific purchasing process. These processes may range from being somewhat structured, but relatively informal to very structured with very formal steps or stages. Whatever the case is for your customers, your sales process should align with your customer's purchasing process. The more closely coordinated those two processes are the more effective and efficient you will be. That is because you will have more opportunities for engagement and optimal timing and relevancy for your interactions.

Seek to fully understand your customer's purchasing process including the steps, timing, sequence of events, participants, and logistics. Know what initiates their purchasing process. Know what their goals and motivators are for each step. By aligning your sales process accordingly, you can work in a complementary way with your customer rather than having to overcome friction or missed opportunities stemming from lack of alignment.

Identify Each Opportunity to Influence Their Decision

Today, information is readily available, and customers are more educated than ever. Savvy buyers use the internet to do their homework before and throughout their decision-making process. As the sales professional, you must be aware of each opportunity to fully understand, educate, and persuade customers, in live direct interactions as well as in the digital world of online and email.

Application: Effective Sales Process

The factors key to an effective sales process are listed below. Check all factors that if implemented, or better executed will improve your sales process.

Factors:

☐ Goal-Based Selling Process: Steps are defined in the sales process with clear goals for each step that result in an efficient progression through the sales cycle and ultimately result in a closed sale.

    ☐ Disciplined execution.

    ☐ Aligned to customer's purchasing process.

    ☐ Identify each opportunity to interact with and influence the customer.

Describe your customer's purchasing process. <u>What</u> is it and <u>why</u>?

____

____

____

____

Describe your sales process. Identify your opportunities to influence your customer throughout their purchasing process. Include critical steps and the goal(s) for each step:

____

____

____

____

Goals: (what I am trying to achieve)

____

____

____

____

____

Implement an effective Sales Process Objectives: (what I must accomplish to achieve my goals)

____

____

____

____

____

Implement an effective Sales Process Key Performance Indicators: (how I will measure what I am achieving)

____

____

____

____

____

Implement an effective Sales Process Data, Reports, and Resources: (information and tools I need)

____

____

____

____

____

Taking into consideration the factors essential to an effective sales process, and those factors that impact me most, my strategy to improve my sales process is:

____

____

____

____

____

____

____

Tactics – the <u>actions</u> I will take when I implement my sales process strategies include:

I will (action):   *by (timeline):*

____

____

____

____

____

____

____

____

____

____

Chapter 14: Pipeline Management Strategies

When we discussed the sales pipeline earlier the focus was on understanding what a healthy pipeline is, and the revenue potential of high-probability opportunities that are needed to ensure that you can meet your monthly and annual new sales revenue requirements.

Let's shift our attention to managing your pipeline effectively. Good pipeline management has four important parameters. The first parameter is analyzing and targeting opportunities, the second parameter is the addition of opportunities to your pipeline. The third parameter is opportunity progression through your pipeline, and the fourth parameter is closing your pipeline opportunities and doing so within your intended timeline.

Your pipeline should be a dynamic flow of opportunities. New opportunities are consistently added, opportunities are developed and matured, and then opportunities ultimately exit your pipeline when you have closed them.

Of course, some opportunities will not close as expected and others are lost due to circumstances beyond your control. Other opportunities are ones you may purposefully deprioritize or even abandon when it becomes clear that the opportunity has low value, will not progress, or when the timeline to closure is extended too far into the future. Whatever the case, opportunities should not sit and stagnate in your pipeline.

What are the key benchmarks that confirm your pipeline management skills are up to par? To answer this question let's first consider the goals for each pipeline parameter, starting with the analysis and targeting of opportunities.

The goal of your analysis and targeting efforts is to identify those opportunities that are most promising and represent the most potential new sales revenue. If this sounds familiar it is because it is also the first step in the Goal-Based Selling Sales Process that was discussed earlier. The relationship between your sales process and your pipeline is inseparable. That is, your sales pipeline is a direct result of your sales process. For that reason, building your sales pipeline and the first steps in your sales process are the same.

What are your goals for adding new opportunities to your pipeline? New pipeline opportunities should be routinely and consistently added to your pipeline. That means new opportunities should be added weekly as an ideal, or monthly at a minimum. New pipeline opportunities should each represent high revenue potential such that when your new opportunities are added together, they should equal 3X-4X your monthly sales goals.

The goal for progressing sales opportunities through your pipeline is to fully develop and advance the opportunity through each necessary stage of the selling cycle promptly and timely. The definition of "timely" may differ depending on your product and its typical sales cycle. Your goal should be to advance opportunities, from the time they enter your pipeline to closure, within the timeline that is typical for your product's sales cycle and according to when closes must occur to meet monthly revenue goals.

What should your goal be for closing? Every sales professional worth their salt wants to close every single opportunity. That is a given, but what should be your minimal acceptable closing ratio? That is, of the opportunities that enter your pipeline, what percentage of them should ultimately close?

Your industry and your organization have an average close ratio. At worst, your closing ratio should meet those measures. Your closing ratio goal will be raised beyond organizational averages according to your desire to perform at your very best and perform at the top of your peer group.

Now let's focus on the skills required for building and managing your pipeline. Like any other professional skill set, pipeline management skills can be developed, honed, and improved. And it is well worth the time and energy invested in doing so because how you build and manage your pipeline directly impacts your goal attainment and your ability to consistently perform at a high level.

Your pipeline of opportunities is the direct result and the tangible evidence of your sales process. Your pipeline is also a reflection of your focus, priorities, and selling skills. Therefore, your pipeline (and how you manage it) provides insights into those selling skills that are strong and the selling skills you can improve upon. Your pipeline management is an important means of self-evaluation and self-managing sales performance.

The essential skillsets related to each pipeline stage are illustrated below (Figure 17.1). These lists of skillsets are meant to be representative, not necessarily exhaustive. Your specific sales process may differ slightly and emphasize certain skills. Regardless, you can see that several skills impact your pipeline at each stage.

In building and managing your pipeline, where do you excel and where is it that you struggle? Do you consistently analyze and target the best and most promising new revenue opportunities? Once those new opportunities are identified are you able to qualify and quantify them and add enough of them to have a healthy pipeline? Do you develop and progress the opportunities through your sales cycle stages efficiently? Does your closing ratio enable you to hit or exceed your monthly and annual goals?

Figure 17.1

Skills:

- Analysis
- Technical
- Goal setting
- Translating information into strategy & tactics
- Observation
- Territory mgmt
- Account mgmt
- Time mgmt
- Call planning

- Relationship building
- Probing
- Listening
- Verbal & non-verbal communication
- Emotional intelligence
- Problem solving
- Product positioning
- Presentation skills

- Aligning solutions to needs wants & desires
- Influence & persuasion
- Objection handling
- Market and competitive product knowledge
- Administrative

Add to previous:
- Project mgmt.
- Leadership
- Train & in-service
- *Trial closing
- Consensus building

Add to previous:
- *Closing skills
- Logistics
- Customer service & support

Analyze & Target → Opportunity Identified / Created → Present Product / Demo → Product Trial / Evaluation → Stakeholders Decide → Close / Implement

Additions **Progression of opportunities through key sales process milestones** **Closes**

Application: Pipeline Management Skills

What skills have you identified that, if improved, will empower you to perform more effectively and faster?

The factors listed below are key to good pipeline management and ultimately, closed business. Check all factors that represent an opportunity to improve your pipeline management.

Factors:

- ☐ Build and maintain a healthy pipeline.
- ☐ Pipeline additions are made consistently and sufficient to meet monthly and annual goals.
- ☐ Opportunities are cultivated so they progress through the pipeline promptly and timely.
- ☐ Opportunities are closed routinely, within the expected timeline, and with sufficient new sales revenue such that monthly quotas are met, and overall sales revenue growth attains annual quota.
- ☐ Your closing ratio meets or exceeds organizational standards.
- ☐ Your closing ratio meets or exceeds your personal performance goal, beyond organizational standards.
- ☐ Opportunities do not sit and stagnate in the pipeline.
- ☐ The pipeline is used as a self-assessment barometer.

Notes:

____

____

____

____

____

____

My growth objective is:

____

____

____

____

____

Therefore, a healthy pipeline in my sales environment is (describe):

____

____

____

____

____

Pipeline **Additions** – Weekly / Monthly Goals	Pipeline **Closes** – Weekly / Monthly Goals

Notes:

____

____

____

____

Closing Ratio/Pipeline Management <u>Goals:</u> (what I am trying to achieve)

____

____

____

____

Closing Ratio/Pipeline Management <u>Objectives</u>: (what I must accomplish to achieve my goals)

____

____

____

____

Closing Ratio/Pipeline Management <u>Key Performance Indicators</u>: (how I will measure what I am achieving)

____

____

____

____

Closing Ratio/Pipeline Management <u>Data, Reports, and Resources</u>: (information and tools I need)

____

____

____

____

Taking into consideration the factors essential to raising my closing ratio via good pipeline management, and those factors that impact me most, my strategy to improve my pipeline management is:

____

____

____

____

____

____

____

____

Tactics – the <u>*actions*</u> *I will take when I implement my pipeline management strategies include:*

I will (action):   *by (timeline):*

____

____

____

____

____

____

____

____

Chapter 15: Increase the Quantity of Sales Opportunities

Increasing the quantity of sales opportunities will increase your results provided all other success factors remain the same.

Increasing the quantity of your sales opportunities begins with your attitude and outlook. In the profession of selling, it is common to hear one's attitude and actions described as either a "hunter" or "farmer." Hunters are those who are more focused on proactively and aggressively seeking out new customer opportunities. The term farmer is used to describe those who focus mainly on growing sales by developing existing customers.

Both approaches have merit, and both can be successful. However, accelerated, and sustained sales revenue growth will at some point require new customers. If hunting is not your natural inclination, then you must consciously choose to make the pursuit of new customers a portion, or a bigger portion of your strategic sales plan.

The key question is what will help you to initiate more sales opportunities? Do you need to "do your homework" by digging deeper in your reports to identify more potential sales opportunities? Do you simply need to make new sales opportunities more of a priority? Or do you need to improve the skills that will help you generate more sales opportunities?

Analyzing and prioritizing sales opportunities is fundamental to increasing the quantity of sales opportunities. If you do not already have a strong understanding of the factors that yield high-value, high-potential sales opportunities then you should look more deeply at your very best existing customers. What are the common characteristics that your finest, highest revenue-producing current customers share? Use those characteristics as benchmarks in your data analysis and territory analysis to identify potential customers who share those same characteristics.

How you manage your time, and your territory will also facilitate an increased quantity of sales opportunities if you allocate time and attention appropriately. You must make finding new sales opportunities (prospecting) a priority. Set a specific goal for the number of new sales opportunities, then specifically allocate time and territory coverage sufficient to meet your goal.

Skills and abilities including analysis, targeting, prospecting, observation, probing, and listening are indispensable to creating more sales opportunities, along with curiosity and business acumen. Learning more and knowing more about your customers and prospective customers leads to opportunities you can capitalize on. Their challenges, aspirations, needs, and wants prompt fruitful conversation about your solutions. Cultivating relationships with stakeholders including end users, decision-makers and decision influencers creates the trust and familiarity that open doors. Also, if you sell equipment or machinery, don't overlook those who maintain and repair that equipment. They can be an excellent source of information including what is being used currently, reliability, problems, maintenance, and repair costs, etc.

Lastly, do not overlook the value of leads and referrals. Leads provided by your organization should be followed up on quickly while customer interest is high. If you don't get leads, or if you don't get many leads from your organization don't despair. Referrals from your customers are just as good, if not better.

Testimonials and customer success stories are worth their weight in gold. Ask for them, keep them in a binder, and use them whenever you can. If your customers are happy with you and your product, ask them to recommend others for you to speak with and have them pave the way for you with an introduction.

Application: Increasing Quantity of Sales Opportunities

Factors key to increasing the quantity of your sales opportunities are listed below. Check all factors that represent an opportunity to increase the quantity of your sales opportunities.

Factors:

- ☐ Hunter mentality.
- ☐ Prospecting as a priority.
- ☐ Target analysis, identification, and prioritization.
- ☐ Effective use of research, reports, data, and sales support.
- ☐ Time management.
- ☐ Territory management.
- ☐ Building and leveraging stakeholder relationships.
- ☐ Lead generation / referrals.
- ☐ Ability to create and / or uncover opportunities.

Notes:

Increase the quantity of sales opportunities <u>Goals:</u> (what I am trying to achieve)

____

____

____

____

Increase the quantity of sales opportunities <u>Objectives</u>: (what I must accomplish to achieve my goals)

____

____

____

____

____

Increase the quantity of sales opportunities <u>Key Performance Indicators</u>: (how I will measure what I am achieving)

____

____

____

____

Increase the quantity of sales opportunities <u>Data, Reports, and Resources</u>: (information and tools I need)

____

____

____

____

____

Taking into consideration the factors essential to increasing the number of sales opportunities, and those factors that impact me most, my strategy to increase the number of sales opportunities is:

____

____

____

____

____

____

____

____

Tactics – the <u>actions</u> I will take when I implement my strategies to increase the quantity of sales opportunities include:

I will (action):   *by (timeline):*

____

____

____

____

____

____

____

____

Chapter 16: Probing Strategy

Probing skills are often thought of as the various techniques used for asking questions. These include techniques such as open probes, closed probes, and so on. That definition of probing skills is accurate but incomplete. Sales professionals do need an arsenal of probing techniques to be their most effective, but what is often left out of the definition of probing skills is the key skill of developing an effective probing strategy.

Building an effective probing strategy is critical to your success. Your probing strategy is how you coordinate and utilize your various probing techniques to efficiently accomplish certain goals in a selling conversation. An effective probing strategy means you are not just asking questions, it means you are asking the right questions.

Why do we probe? We probe to discover, learn, and understand. We also probe to confirm information. We probe to cause the other person to contemplate, speculate, and share insights beyond a simple question-and-answer dynamic.

The key to creating a powerful probing strategy is to first establish specific goals for your interaction. The time to build your probing strategy is when you are planning your call. Consider the following - What is it that you need to learn and understand from the other person? At what stage in your selling process do you need to know it? What insights do you need? Are there key inflection points you wish for the other person to ponder and reflect upon? How and when will you pose the question or questions to accomplish this goal? By first identifying your probing goals your probing strategy comes more into focus.

An effective probing strategy must be efficient. By efficient, I mean your probing strategy should include the fewest number of probes necessary to provide you with the information or response that you seek. Customers will not tolerate being interrogated or answering an endless string of questions. That is why pre-planning is so important, as is gathering as much information as possible before your meeting. Consider what you can learn ahead of time via an internet search or from other data sources. And what can you learn from others before your meeting?

Plan your full probing strategy, but also have a backup plan. Having decided the questions you will ask, think about how you will prioritize your questions if your time is limited, and you can't ask all the questions you originally planned. If you can only ask 3-4 questions, what would they be? What if you could only ask one? This is where knowing what you need to uncover or confirm, the personality and typical behaviors of the other person(s), and the amount of time you expect to have (along with a time-compressed plan B) is crucial to your probing strategy.

Early in a sales conversation, your focus is on discovery. You must learn and understand the full scope and scale of the customer's needs. You need to know "what" and "why".

A great way to economize questions while encouraging your customer to share volumes of information is to use phrases such as "tell me about…" or "describe…". Then, listen carefully to what they say. Also, listen to what they do not say. Your customer's verbal and non-verbal responses are equally educational and revealing. Be sensitive to body language, tone, and voice inflection which may indicate skepticism, problems, areas of interest and other "hot buttons."

When there are multiple people involved in the conversation or sales process, be sure to communicate with each person. Don't assume they all share the same viewpoints and priorities. Often it is true that when more people are involved in a decision or purchasing process, the more likely it is there is discrepancy in their individual needs, viewpoints, and concerns. Your goal is to discover, learn, and understand.

As you learn and gain understanding, you can begin to formulate how you will position and differentiate your product. Your probing strategy should clarify for you how you can best align your product to the customer needs and goals you uncovered. Also uncover why the customer would purchase your product and why they should purchase your product.

The reasons why the customer would and should purchase your product tie directly into all the information they have shared with you, and by getting as much information as possible, especially the motivations that are behind their need, goal, and priorities you will be able to identify and prioritize the key points you will build your presentation upon.

As you progress through the selling conversation and gain knowledge, you need to confirm what you have learned and what you understand. This is to ensure that you are fully aligned with your customer. Be certain your probing strategy includes questions designed to confirm, clarify, and expound as needed.

Your probing strategy must go far beyond simply gaining basic information. It is paramount to your success to understand customer motivations and reasoning. Understanding implications are especially important. For example, what would happen if the customer does decide to purchase your product? What would happen if the decision was not to purchase the product? What are the implications?

Implication questions provide you insights into the customer's consequences (pros and cons) if their goal is or is not met, or the problem at hand is or is not resolved successfully. Consequences are strong emotional drivers that can help you overcome resistance or inertia.

What goes best with probing skills is listening skills. Critical listening is more than simply hearing; it requires focused attention and active engagement. Listen with your ears and eyes to best interpret how body language and voice inflection interact. Does what you observe confirm or disagree with the words being spoken?

Listen not only for what is said but also for what is not said. Both carry important messages that help to paint the entire picture and provide you with a more comprehensive understanding. If your sales process involves a series of meetings be alert to any lack of consistency in your conversations. The information your customer shares, questions they ask, and the overall tone in verbal and non-verbal communications should remain consistent unless something new has entered the equation and changed the dynamics. Everything carries a message and where there is change there is also a reason behind that change. You must catch the change when it occurs and then seek to clarify and understand.

Be aware of speech patterns. For instance, notice when generalities are used in a response, rather than specifics. Generalities are often less trustworthy than specifics. When you begin to hear generalities, it is an opportunity for you to probe further and clarify what you have heard, so that you are confident in the information you are gathering and that your understanding of the information is accurate. The use of qualifying or positioning phrases should also cause you to probe further to clarify the information you are receiving.

There are times when you ask a question, and your customer takes extra time – perhaps too much time before providing their response. You can tell they are thinking through how they want to respond. It is a good thing when your customer is trying to thoughtfully consider how to best provide a full and clear response. On the other hand, if the extra time taken was to carefully wordsmith their response, you should be wary. In those situations, be aware in case there is an attempt to deceive or mislead you. If you encounter such a response, be sure to probe further and clarify anything that is unclear to you.

It should be part of your probing strategy to clarify common words and phrases that may be open to interpretation. Why is it so important to clarify common words and phrases? It is because there is so much opportunity for misconceptions and miscommunications.

We naturally probe when we hear something we don't understand or when we hear something we're not familiar with. However, when we hear a word such as "many, often, or all the time" we don't question them because we know what all those words mean. Or do we?

What we should do is probe to clarify and confirm how the other person is using the term in question. We should probe to understand how many is "many?" How often is "often?" Is "all the time" really every single time?

When should we probe to clarify common words? We should clarify whenever such words are used in the description of the customer's needs, goals, or problems. We should probe to clarify when customers include such words when they describe buying criteria or priorities. We should probe to clarify when customers respond to things we've said or questions we have asked. In short, whenever it is important to have a clear understanding of what our customer is communicating, we should clarify any words or phrases that are nonspecific or vague.

As an example, let us suppose you were buying a car and I was the salesperson. Let us further suppose that you told me one of the attributes you wanted in your next car was that it would be fun to drive.

I would immediately know what my definition of "fun" is, but would I know with certainty that you defined "fun" the same way? If we both defined "fun" differently, how much opportunity would there be for me to misinterpret how you were using the word?

Let's say your definition of fun was packing the car full of friends and food so you could go to the beach. On the other hand, my definition of fun was driving in a spirited fashion through curvy canyon roads. If I had a spectrum of cars that I could show you, including large vehicles with plenty of seats and storage and high-performance sports cars, what car might I be inclined to show you? What car might I show you if I had clarified the kind of fun you had in mind?

Listen carefully to the words your customers use. Uncovering and understanding information is the bedrock of your ability to position your product accurately and communicate its most important benefits impactfully for your prospective customer. Having a probing strategy and following your probing strategy faithfully will provide you with the information and understanding that you need.

Application: Effective Probing Strategy

Below are the factors essential to an effective probing strategy. Check all factors that if performed more consistently or more effectively, would improve your probing strategy.

Factors:

- ☐ A well-conceived probing strategy is pre-planned and created for each sales call.
- ☐ A backup probing strategy is pre-planned and created for each sales call.
- ☐ My probing strategy is efficient – I gain all the information I need with an economy of probes.
- ☐ My probing strategy results in a full understanding of the customer's current solution, why they chose it and continue to use it presently.
- ☐ My probing strategy consistently uncovers customer:
  - ☐ Problems, goals, needs, and wants.
  - ☐ Decision making process, timelines, stakeholders, decision makers, and decision influencers.
- ☐ Motivations, root causes, and priorities behind their problems, goals, needs, and wants.
- ☐ My probing strategy provides me with deep customer insights that result from asking customers to speculate and describe implications related to problems, concerns, goals, outcomes, and purchasing decisions.
- ☐ My probing strategy consistently provides the customer information and insights I need to align my solution to their needs, wants, and priorities. I can accurately position and present my solution in a more compelling way because of what I have learned.
- ☐ Part of my probing strategy is to clarify words, phrases, and speech patterns that, if not clarified might otherwise lead to miscommunication.
- ☐ Listening and observation are integral to effective probing. I employ critical listening skills and am a skilled observer of verbal and non-verbal communications. I probe to clarify when appropriate.

☐   I am disciplined and execute my probing strategy as I have designed it.

What would enable you to make your probing strategy even more effective?

____

____

____

____

____

____

____

____

____

Notes:

____

____

____

____

____

Probing Strategy _Goals:_ (what I am trying to achieve)

____

____

____

____

____

Probing Strategy _Objectives:_ (what I must accomplish to achieve my goals)

____

____

____

____

____

Probing Strategy _Key Performance Indicators_: (how I will measure what I am achieving)

____

____

____

____

____

Probing Strategy _Data, Reports, and Resources_: (information and tools I need)

____

____

____

____

____

Taking into consideration the factors essential to an effective probing strategy, and those factors that impact me most, I will improve my probing strategy by:

____

____

____

____

____

____

____

____

____

Tactics – the <u>actions</u> I will take to improve my probing strategy include:

I will (action):   *by (timeline):*

____

____

____

____

____

____

____

____

____

____

Chapter 17: Increase Qualified Sales Opportunities

Increasing the number of sales opportunities is important but no sales opportunity will close and produce new revenue for you if it is not a properly *qualified* opportunity. A qualified sales opportunity means you have confirmed that a legitimate opportunity exists. Your product can meet your prospect's need, and they can purchase it (provided that is what they choose to do) within a timeline that enables you to meet your monthly and annual new sales revenue goals and quota.

A qualified opportunity justifies the time and energy required to develop the opportunity whereas much time and effort will be wasted if a bona fide opportunity does not exist. It is vital to qualify the opportunity as early in the sales process as possible to save yourself and your prospect time and frustration.

Probing skills and an effective probing strategy enable you to qualify opportunities efficiently. Qualifying the opportunity should be done as early in your sales process as possible so that you are investing your time on closable opportunities rather than wasting time where you have no chance of success.

Qualifying the opportunity involves understanding your prospect's situation. What is their problem and why is the problem occurring? Can your product resolve the issue or enable them to meet their goal? If so, how? You need a complete picture so that you are certain you can provide a solution.

Having a complete picture means you have a full understanding of your prospect, their business, and their need. You have identified the decision-maker and any other decision influencers. You know their purchasing process, their product selection criteria, as well as the weight and priority of the selection criteria. You and your prospective customer have a full and mutual understanding of the implications of their decision and potential solutions.

You also know your prospect's motivations, including the weight and priority of their motivations. When all factors are combined, you are confident that what you will provide in product and services aligns with everything that is important to your prospect.

The prospect must also be able to purchase your product. That means they have the authority, and they have the necessary funds. No contracts or other obstacles prevent them from doing business with you and their purchasing timeline meets your time requirements.

When you have taken in all the required information, and you are confident in your solution as well as your prospective customer's ability to purchase it then proceed with determination and tenacity. You are pursuing a fully qualified opportunity!

Application: Qualifying Your Sales Opportunities

Factors most important to qualifying sales opportunities are provided below. Check all factors that represent an opportunity for you to better qualify your sales opportunities.

Factors:

- ☐ Your prospect's current situation is understood, along with <u>why</u> there is an opportunity for improvement.
- ☐ Your probing strategy has fully illuminated the opportunity for improvement. You clearly understand how and why your solution will provide what your customer needs to resolve their problem and/or accomplish their goal.
- ☐ Stakeholders, including relevant end users, decision makers and decision influencers have been identified.
- ☐ The ability and means to purchase your solution, if desired, are present. These include:
  - ☐ Authority
  - ☐ Funds
  - ☐ Other
    - ☐ RFP
    - ☐ Contracts
- ☐ Decision Maker purchase criteria need and/or desire is mutually understood…along with <u>weight</u> and <u>implications</u> of each.
- ☐ Stakeholder purchase criteria need and/or desire is aligned with product/service.
- ☐ Stakeholder motivations mutually understood.
- ☐ Stakeholder motivations aligned with product/service.
- ☐ Decision Maker timeline for purchase is mutually understood and is optimal.

____

____

____

Increase qualified sales opportunities <u>Goals:</u> (what I am trying to achieve)

____

____

____

____

____

Increase qualified sales opportunities <u>Objectives</u>: (what I must accomplish to achieve my goals)

____

____

____

____

____

Increase qualified sales opportunities <u>Key Performance Indicators</u>: (how I will measure what I am achieving)

____

____

____

____

Increase qualified sales opportunities <u>Data, Reports, and Resources</u>: (information and tools I need)

____

____

____

____

Taking into consideration the factors essential to qualifying sales opportunities, and those factors that impact me most, my strategy to increase my efficiency in qualifying sales opportunities is:

____

____

____

____

____

____

____

Tactics – the <u>actions</u> I will take when qualifying my sales opportunities include:

I will (action):   *by (timeline):*

____

____

____

____

____

____

____

____

____

Chapter 18: Overcoming Objections

Effectively handling objections boils down to two things. One is the technique(s) you use to overcome the objection. The second is the quality, validity, and credibility of your response, whether that information is data or other forms of proof and substantiation. Successfully overcoming objections requires both a good technique and a valid response. However, either your technique or the information you provide – or both - can be the source of your downfall when you are unsuccessful in overcoming objections.

There is another consideration as well. You must be able to overcome objections in such a way that you remain professional and likable in the eyes of your prospective customer. Does your customer want to continue moving toward the sale once the objection has been discussed? The old saying "win the battle, lose the war" comes to mind. It can easily be applied to the salesperson who is "right" and successfully proves their point but loses the sale anyway because they have alienated their customer. Don't allow yourself to get into an argument with your customer! Self-discipline is a key in overcoming objections, keeping the selling conversation productive, and the customer engaged.

As a quick aside, be sure you are not interpreting customer questions as objections. Questions indicate customer interest and involvement. Questions should be taken as a positive and therefore welcomed and encouraged.

Similarly, objections are not "bad." Objections can easily represent an opportunity to provide customers information that is very important to them as they consider a purchase. If the customer did not voice their concern, then a vital piece of information may have been missed. Thank the customer for voicing their concern in such cases so that the information can be delivered, or clarified, and the sale can be kept on track. Treat objections as an opportunity to better communicate exactly what your customer needs to know, rather than a harbinger of a lost sales opportunity.

Indifference *is* bad because it indicates your customer has no interest in what you are offering, and they are not considering a purchase. When you encounter genuine indifference, you must consider whether the opportunity was qualified accurately. Recall that a qualified opportunity means there is a real need that your product can meet. A product should not be presented before fully qualifying the opportunity.

A deal killer that should not be confused with an objection is when a criterion exists and must be met before a sale can be agreed upon. As a simple example, let us say a customer requires lumber in twelve-foot boards. If you are only able to provide eight-foot boards then your customer has a purchase criterion you are unable to meet. That is not an objection to overcome. You can either meet the criteria or you cannot. Criterion can include product or service specifications, delivery schedules, and so on. Criteria should be uncovered as part of your qualifying process, not discovered during your product presentation.

We all know that encountering objections is par for the course for every sales professional. The good thing is that there are only so many objections that you will encounter, and you will quickly learn what objections you will receive. Within the first few months of selling a product, you will have encountered all or nearly all the objections that you ever will hear when selling a given product. Collect the objections you receive. Write them down, along with responses and any associated proof sources. Do this in a quiet moment when you are not under the pressure of a live conversation. You can then carefully and thoughtfully determine your best responses. Then, practice, practice, practice until you can confidently and smoothly overcome each objection.

You will get to the point where you can anticipate the objections. You can decide whether to take them on proactively during your presentation and systematically overcome them, or you can leave them for the customer to bring up and then address them. The point is, when you are fully prepared and appropriately armed, you can smile inside all the while knowing you have a slam dunk response.

For the objections that you frequently encounter, build a probing strategy to proactively discover and confirm if the suspected objection is a concern for the customer you are speaking with. If you strongly suspect or know the objection exists, don't avoid it, hit it head-on. By anticipating and being proactive you can provide your best response and proof as part of your presentation. The caveat here is to confirm the objection first. If you try to overcome an objection the customer truly does not have, it can seem as though you are being defensive. It may create questions in the customer's mind and raise concerns that were not there originally.

No matter what you do to prepare yourself it is likely that at some point you will encounter an objection that you are not fully prepared to address. A temptation, especially when you are under the pressure of the moment, is to guess or share information that may be incomplete. Resist the temptation! Your credibility is vital to your success so don't compromise it with a response that is not the best it can be.

Instead, indicate that in the interest of providing the most accurate and complete information possible, you would like to gather some resources so you can then provide a more thorough answer. This approach enables you to address the objection with a much more cohesive and thoughtful response. You will feel less pressured because you will have done your homework and compiled everything needed to be at your best. Your customer should also appreciate your extra effort to provide full and accurate information. When you do follow up, do it as quickly as possible so that you do not lose the window of opportunity. If possible, follow up in person rather than with an email or anything else that is not a live interaction.

Some situations should cause you to pause and reflect on why they are occurring or recurring. One such situation is when you hear the same objection that you have heard many times before, yet you continue to struggle with an effective response. It is okay to be surprised once with a new objection that you have not encountered previously. But before you encounter that objection again, take time to review the objection and determine how you will successfully handle it the next time that it is presented to you. Don't be caught unprepared a second time!

Another situation that should raise a caution flag is when you routinely receive numerous objections when presenting your solution. When that occurs, consider that you may not be presenting your product in a way that is compelling for your prospective customer. It is necessary to better align how you position and present your product relative to your customer's needs, wants, and priorities. That points back to probing skills, probing strategy, listening skills, and confirming that you are truly understanding all that your customer needs you to understand.

Focus on the skills that will help you improve so that you can better position and present your product in the future. If you are gathering the right information, understanding your customer's needs well, and then effectively presenting your solution compellingly then you should not be getting a large volume of objections.

When you encounter an objection, it can be tempting to respond immediately. That is often a poor technique because by doing so, you can seem defensive or argumentative. Instead, view the objection as an opportunity to learn more. Ask your customer to shed some additional light on the subject. Probe to better understand what is behind your customer's objection. By doing this you will have a more complete comprehension of the objection and why they are voicing it. Also, you will have more time to prepare your best response.

Good probes can be: "Help me understand what you mean…" or, "Tell me what prompts your question…" or, "Tell me more about that…" Get as much information as your customer will share. Then ask, "what else concerns you?" or, "what else can I answer for you?" Listen to each response until your customer has no more to add.

By asking the questions, your customer will provide you with more information to work with. Listen carefully to their response. There are many reasons why a customer may object. Your goal is to understand why they are objecting and what the nature of their objection is. Get as much information as possible before offering your response.

When your customer has provided a full response (be patient and don't interrupt!) thank them for the additional insights. Then, paraphrase back to them what they said to confirm you understood exactly what they were conveying to you. Only then should you respond to their objection. You will have much more information to work with and your customer will be impressed with how much you care about their concern (because you listened and confirmed your understanding by paraphrasing it back to them). They will be more inclined to listen to you as well when you respond to them.

Some customers simply misunderstand, or they are misinformed or confused. When you ask them to further explain their objection their misunderstanding or confusion will become obvious. You can then provide them with the correct information, thus alleviating their concern. When you have clarified the information be sure to confirm their concern has been removed.

Sometimes customers object because they doubt what you're telling them. What they are asking for is more information and proof. Ask, listen, and learn! When you have a full understanding of their objection it will be clear to you that they need additional information and proof of what you're telling them. This is an excellent time to introduce or review the proof sources you have that are relevant to your customer's area of concern. As when customers are misinformed or misunderstand, be sure to confirm their concern has been removed after you provide additional information and proof.

There are other times when your product has a limitation or even a deficit in one area when compared to the customer's ideal solution, or a competitive product. When you ask the customer for more detail, they will often give you an indication of how to offset the limitation to minimize the impact on the overall decision. Going back to the information you gained earlier, you can highlight other benefits your solution provides that may outweigh the limitation, especially when you look at the problem and solution in its entirety.

Let's get to the one objection everyone hears at one time or another. That is the pricing objection. What do you do when your customer is fixated on price or even says your product is too expensive? That's right! Don't get defensive or flustered. Be prepared.

Pricing discussions that occur right off the bat rarely result in a positive outcome. When the conversation is all about price before you have identified needs and built value in your solution, you will seldom win. You will not salvage the conversation or the sale unless your product is the least expensive option.

Resist the urge to respond with pricing information immediately. Instead, you can say "Let's both agree that pricing is always an important consideration, and we will review the pricing in detail. But let's also agree that in addition to price, other considerations will determine if the solution is the right one for you. Let's find out if I have a solution that provides you with exactly what you're looking for. If not, then the price is irrelevant anyway. Tell me about the other factors that will go into your decision…"

Now you can proceed with your probing strategy to uncover needs, priorities, and decision criteria. Focus the conversation on all the other factors and how your product provides benefits and value considering those factors. The advantage in postponing answering the price question is that you will have been able to create value for your product rather than have it treated as a simple commodity.

You may also ask if you can suggest a few things to consider in their purchasing decision if your customer is overlooking important factors. That allows you to introduce some new decision factors and criteria where appropriate.

Only after discussing all the factors should you reveal the price. That way you have gained the opportunity to have a selling conversation where you can align your solution to their needs and differentiate your product rather than just focusing on a pricing discussion. That gives your customer the chance to make a more informed purchasing decision and you the opportunity to earn a sale!

If pricing is brought up as a concern or objection later in the conversation after you have fully understood their needs and presented your product, you must handle the pricing question more directly. But first, ask questions and listen to their response.

"Help me understand what makes you say that," or, "How far above your budget is the price?" Have them identify the gap. What do they think the price should be, and why? Perhaps they have a rational and valid reason for concern. Or perhaps they are protesting but have no basis for doing so. By asking the questions you get more information with which to proceed more effectively.

Sometimes customers offer a pricing objection because they truly don't have the budget for your solution. If they have the budget, then they may be challenging you to see if you will lower the price. Or they may be trying to determine if the value your product provides is worth the price to them. Show them that the value is there, and you will earn their business.

What do you do when a customer is adamant about something they perceive as a negative concerning your product or your organization? Is there a way to gain a temporary truce so that you can introduce information that can help to change their mind? There is!

When I began working with one organization, I quickly found many customers who were passionately opposed to that organization due to some things that had taken place in the past. As a result, some customers would not even consider the product I was selling. When I encountered those customers, rather than walk away defeated, I posed a very simple, yet effective question.

I indicated I had some information that pertained to the very concern they had raised. I asked them if they would be willing to at least review and consider the information with an open mind. More often than not, they answered "yes." That provided me the opportunity to present all the information I had pertaining to their concern while they were trying to "keep an open mind" and consider all the facts. This often led to a very open and fruitful discussion. Many would ultimately agree that "whatever did happen" was in the past and that they were willing to provide an honest opportunity to move forward with a more collaborative approach.

The key to this approach is humility and patience. In gaining agreement that the customer would "be willing to consider additional information with an open mind" it allowed me to have a calm and thorough discussion and begin to build trust. It can work for you as well.

The last objection I'll mention is one of the most difficult to handle: the hidden objection. What makes the hidden objection difficult to handle is that you cannot successfully address an objection or concern until you get it out in the open. If you do not get it into the open, you may lose the opportunity and never understand why.

When you sense something is holding the customer back you can say "it seems there is something that is making you hesitant – what it that?" or "It seems like you have a question. Help me understand what that is." Once you surface their previously hidden objection you can then handle it just as you would any other objection.

Now, let's talk about the information and resources that you will utilize to overcome objections. That is, what proof sources do you have that back up your claims and provide additional details on your products? The best proof sources are detailed and credible. Examples are proof sources generated from expert third-party resources such as a respected industry expert or even a current customer that is known by your prospective customer. Have your proof sources organized so you can quickly access them when needed.

The best approach when providing proof sources is to present proof in printed form or pictures rather than just your spoken word. Printed documents are much more credible and convincing than an unsubstantiated verbal response, even if your response is accurate.

Product reviews and customer feedback are excellent forms of social proof. If this applies to your product and selling scenario, bring samples to show and discuss.

The ultimate response to a concern or objection is a product demonstration that provides the direct evidence and proof needed to overcome the objection. Show them! Have your customer see and experience your product for themselves. As they say, the proof is in the pudding.

Whatever the objection was, once you have addressed it do not assume that it is resolved in your customer's mind until they confirm that is the case. Ask the question! Did your response provide the information they needed to feel confident in moving forward? If not, why not? What else would help? Only when you have a full confirmation should you proceed with the selling conversation.

The last thing I'll mention about overcoming objections is the opportunity/responsibility you have to communicate customer feedback to your organization. There are times when there is a real deficit that is negatively impacting your success and your organization's success. You are the critical intersection between your organization and its customer base. As a member of the sales team, you are closer to your customer and your market than anyone else in the organization. Your feedback is an integral part of resolving issues and obstacles between the two parties.

When the need arises, engage Management, Marketing, Engineering, Customer Service, and anyone else who needs awareness so that issues can be resolved, products can be refined or redesigned, service levels or terms and conditions can be improved to restore your ability to compete successfully for business. In such cases your customers win, your organization wins, and you win. The best way to overcome an objection is to eliminate it, and at times, you are uniquely positioned to do just that!

Application: Effectively Overcoming Objections

Below are the factors essential to effectively overcoming objections. Check all factors that, if performed more consistently or more effectively, would improve your ability to overcome objections.

Factors:

- ☐ A variety of effective objection handling techniques is possessed and utilized successfully for the type of objections encountered.
- ☐ The quality, validity, and credibility of responses and proof sources effectively overcomes the objections encountered.
- ☐ Professionalism and likeability are preserved while overcoming objections.
- ☐ Questions are distinguished from true objections and responded to appropriately.
- ☐ Frequently encountered objections are known, collected, and have prepared responses .
- ☐ Objection responses are crafted, practiced, and delivered effectively with confidence.
- ☐ Objections are minimized or avoided by carefully aligning the product presentation to previously uncovered customer needs, wants, goals, and priorities.
- ☐ Indifference and/or deal-killing criterion are avoided through proper opportunity qualification.
- ☐ Probing is used to understand the objection more fully before providing a response.
- ☐ Price-related objections are avoided or overcome by establishing product value.
- ☐ Hidden objections are detected, successfully surfaced, and overcome.
- ☐ When an objection has been addressed, the customer's satisfaction with the response and readiness to advance the sales conversation is confirmed.
- ☐ Customer needs and concerns are communicated to the organization to eliminate objections.

List the objections and FAQs you most frequently encounter and describe how you can best respond to them including responses and proof sources:

____

____

____

____

____

____

____

____

____

____

____

____

____

____

____

____

____

____

Overcome Objections <u>Goals:</u> (what I am trying to achieve)

____

____

____

____

____

Overcome Objections <u>Objectives:</u> (what I must accomplish to achieve my goals)

____

____

____

____

____

Overcome Objections <u>Key Performance Indicators</u>: (how I will measure what I am achieving)

____

____

____

____

____

Overcome Objections <u>Data, Reports, and Resources</u>: (information and tools I need)

____

____

____

____

____

Taking into consideration the factors essential to effectively overcoming objections, and those factors that impact me most, I will improve my ability to overcome objections by:

____

____

____

____

____

____

____

____

Tactics – the <u>actions</u> I will take to improve my objections handling strategy include:

I will (action):   *by (timeline):*

____

____

____

____

____

____

____

____

____

____

Chapter 19: Gaining Commitment

Gaining commitment is in many ways akin to closing skills, but as a concept, gaining commitment goes beyond just closing and closing skills. Commitment is gained (earned) incrementally through the course of the sales process and is a prerequisite to successfully advancing and closing the sale. As your prospective customer increasingly realizes just how well your solution will help them accomplish their goals, solve their problem, and meet their need, their commitment grows until they are ready to make the final decision when they commit to purchasing your product.

Gaining commitment can begin as soon as you start to interact with your customer. As your customer becomes more familiar with you, your product, and the company you represent, you establish the potential for commitment. As you continue to interact with your customer you can cultivate that potential and earn your customer's support and loyalty.

Commitment builds within your customers as they discover just how well your solution helps them meet their needs. That means you must first gain a deep understanding of your customer and their needs. Only once you have that deep understanding can you best position and present your solution. Otherwise, you will not be successful in building your customer's trust, confidence, and commitment to you or your solution.

Customers can buy into and become committed to three things. Those three things are your product, your company, and you. Any one of these, or combination, can be what earns a level of commitment resulting in the sale.

Customers are not so much committed to a product per se, as they are committed to what they want that product to do for them. They want the product to solve problems, help them accomplish their goals, improve outcomes, and so forth. When prospective customers understand, and especially when they experience how well the product provides or accomplishes what they need the product to do for them, customers become increasingly committed to that product.

Organizations earn customer loyalty and commitment. Customers buy into what the company does, how they do it, and why they do it; what the organization stands for, how the company takes care of its customers, and any number of other reasons that make the company admirable and desirable in the customer's eyes.

Most importantly, you can also earn your customer's commitment. You establish, grow, and cement your customer's commitment to you for all the reasons mentioned above. And especially because of how you help your customers accomplish their goals.

As you navigate the sales process with your customers, recognize how your product, your organization, and you can earn your customer's commitment. As you earn your customer's commitment you will also earn their business. Because you directly interact with your customers, you are the most important influence on them and their purchasing decision. You are More important than the product you sell and the organization at which you work. Earning your customer's commitment to you as a trusted professional resource will have the greatest impact on your ability to successfully sell any product.

Gaining commitment is a process. This is where the concept of incrementalism can be useful. In this context, incrementalism is deliberately and persistently building on each success or advancement toward the goal of securing the sale. Throughout the process, you are gaining small commitments that lead to the ultimate commitment of closing the sale.

Incrementalism can also be used as an account development strategy. The initial goal is to find a starting point for you and your customer to begin doing business together. Then by ensuring your customer experiences excellent results, you steadily earn and secure additional commitment. The results come from using your product and they also come from the superior customer experience you provide. Ensuring customer success paves the way and provides you the opportunity to ask for additional business. In many cases, it is much easier to develop a customer in this way than to earn a very large piece of business all at once.

As you successfully build commitment within your customers an important aspect of advancing the sales process or closing means asking for your customer to make decisions and take specific actions. Two prerequisites must be in place when you make your request. First, be certain that the decision or action you are requesting is within your customer's ability to perform. Second, make sure your customer is ready and willing to do what you are asking of them.

Frustration will result if a customer is asked to do something they are incapable of doing. That scenario can occur in a complex selling environment when your prospective customer has multiple people involved in the sales process. When speaking with a supporter, even someone who is an internal champion for you, only ask them to do what they have authority and the wherewithal to do. This is where understanding roles, responsibilities, and level of authority is critical.

Provided that you have established and cultivated trust and commitment throughout your interaction(s) you should be able to observe and confirm your customer's readiness to make the decision or take the action you request of them. Readiness is evidenced by buying signals that customers communicate verbally and non-verbally. Readiness is also confirmed using trial closes.

Application: Gaining Commitment

Below are the factors essential to gaining commitment. Check all factors that, if accomplished more consistently or more effectively, would improve your ability to gain customer commitment.

Factors:

- ☐ Gaining customer commitment is a goal for every sales call.
- ☐ I gain customer commitment by developing a thorough understanding of their problem or opportunity, along with their desired outcome.
- ☐ Considering customer needs, I gain customer commitment by presenting my solution in a manner that relates to how my solution resolves their problem and/or delivers the desired outcome.
- ☐ I successfully gain customer commitment for my product.
- ☐ I successfully gain customer commitment for my organization.
- ☐ I successfully gain customer commitment for myself as a trusted professional resource.
- ☐ I leverage customer commitment by systematically building on successes that advance the sale to closure.
- ☐ I systematically and purposefully build customer commitment through incremental positive business experiences and outcomes that result in additional growth opportunity.
- ☐ I leverage customer commitment by asking for specific actions and decisions to advance the sale and close the sale.
- ☐ I understand customer roles, responsibilities, and levels of authority. The actions and decisions I ask of them are within my customer's ability to perform.
- ☐ I confirm customer readiness for action by monitoring verbal and non-verbal buying signals and through the use of trial closes.

Gaining Commitment <u>Goals:</u> (what I am trying to achieve)

____

____

____

____

____

Gaining Commitment <u>Objectives:</u> (what I must accomplish to achieve my goals)

____

____

____

____

____

Gaining Commitment <u>Key Performance Indicators</u>: (how I will measure what I am achieving)

____

____

____

____

____

Gaining Commitment <u>Data, Reports, and Resources</u>: (information and tools I need)

____

____

____

____

____

Taking into consideration the factors essential to gaining commitment, and those factors that impact me most, I will improve my ability to gain commitment by:

____

____

____

____

____

____

____

____

Tactics – the <u>actions</u> I will take to improve my ability to gain commitment include:

I will (action):   *by (timeline):*

____

____

____

____

____

____

____

____

____

____

Chapter 20: Decrease the Time Required to Close the Sale and Gain Utilization

Time may be on the Rolling Stones' side, but for us sales professionals, that is rarely the case. The old cliché that time is money is more appropriate for us. Our goal as sales professionals is to reduce the time required to close sales as well as the time required to receive the revenue from those sales.

Of the resources you manage, your time is one of the most precious. You cannot create more time; you can only make better use of the time you have. To maximize your results, you are compelled to use your time efficiently and productively.

Efficient use of time and greater productively starts with your goals. Your goals should dictate your priorities and inform the best use of your time. Ask yourself "is (X activity) in line with my goals or not?" This simple question tells you the importance of the activity. If an activity does not help you reach your goal it is something to deprioritize. In fact, the activity may be something you should not do at all. You gain time by not wasting it on low-priority activities.

Goals and priorities lead you to focus. Relentlessly squeeze out distractions and low priority, time-consuming activities. Dedicate your attention to your top priorities, such as qualified pipeline opportunities so you can actively advance them to closure. Also, consider those prospective customers who are eager and motivated to move forward. Where you have those situations use the natural momentum to your advantage. Capitalize on the situation by doing what is necessary to close the sale quickly.

Be efficient with travel. Route yourself as directly as possible so that you can spend your valuable hours and minutes where they are most required. Get up earlier so that you avoid rush hour traffic. Schedule meetings when customers can dedicate the time required rather than showing up and hoping you can gain a few minutes of their time.

Another way to save time is to build your professional selling skills. A more skilled sales professional will advance the sales process faster, close opportunities faster, and close more effectively. So, by building and polishing your selling skills you save time. Any lagging professional skills are costing you time and they are also costing you money. Do what is needed to bring those skills up to a level where they are contributing to your success and income rather than slowing you down.

The time crunch does not end once the sale is closed. Many sales professionals must coordinate certain logistics such as ordering, shipping, stocking, distribution, training, and any others unique your product. Be aware of what will be required of you so that you can be proactive in supporting those needs. Otherwise, significant time will be lost coordinating all the details and sales will not occur until those details are resolved.

If you have company resources that help by facilitating these processes, use them! The most valuable use of your time is when you are driving sales. If you can hand off certain support activities, then do it!

Below are the factors key to reducing the time required to close the sale and gain product utilization. Check all factors that represent an opportunity to decrease the time required to close opportunities and gain product utilization.

Application: Reduce Time to Close Opportunities and Gain Product Utilization

Factors:

- ☐ Set goals and use goals such as your quota and other strategic deliverables to determine the best use of your time.
    - o Ensure your goals dictate your priorities and activities.
    - o Separate "need to do" from "nice to do" activities.
    - o Deprioritize or eliminate low priority activities.
- ☐ Focus!
    - o On qualified, prioritized opportunities.
    - o Motivated customers = customer goals, priorities, and purchase timeline align strongly with product/services.
    - o Actively manage pipeline opportunities through the sales process.
    - o Territory management is time and travel efficient.
- ☐ Honed selling skills = faster progression through the sales process.
- ☐ Efficiently plan and execute the logistics of ordering, stocking & utilizing.
- ☐ Efficiently plan and execute any required training or in-servicing.
- ☐ Efficient after-sale follow-up.
- ☐ Utilize internal tools & resources (Marketing, Technical, Customer Service, Support Staff).

Notes:

____

____

____

____

Decrease TIME <u>Goals:</u> (what I am trying to achieve)

____

____

____

____

Decrease TIME <u>Objectives</u>: (what I must accomplish to achieve my goals)

____

____

____

____

Decrease TIME <u>Key Performance Indicators</u>: (how I will measure what I am achieving)

____

____

____

____

Decrease TIME <u>Data, Reports, and Resources</u>: (information and tools I need)

____

____

____

____

Taking into consideration the factors essential to decreasing the time required to close the sale and gain utilization, and those factors that impact me most, my strategy to decreasing the time required to close the sale and gain utilization is:

____

____

____

____

____

____

____

____

Tactics – the <u>actions</u> I will take to decrease the time required to close the sale and gain utilization include:

I will (action):   *by (timeline):*

____

____

____

____

____

____

____

____

Chapter 21: Increase the Revenue Potential of Sales Opportunities

It is a better strategy to prioritize opportunities with greater revenue potential over those opportunities with lower revenue potential. Over the many years that I held sales leadership positions, I routinely saw sales professionals spend too much time on low-value opportunities that drained away their time and energy but yielded small revenue returns for their effort. Don't do that! Sell more by focusing on those opportunities with the greatest revenue potential. Each win will produce more revenue and contribute more to your success.

The first step in prioritizing opportunities with greater revenue potential is finding them. Your territory sales reports will readily reveal existing customers who purchase your product in greater volume than other customers. Identify the characteristics that align with greater purchase potential versus lesser potential. Then, using those characteristics you can identify prospective customers with the greatest opportunity.

Other sources that help identify the larger targets include industry reports, internet searches, peers, and other knowledgeable people inside and outside of your organization.

When you are speaking directly with prospective customers you can quantify and confirm their revenue potential in a few ways. Probe and investigate! You may learn the current product unit volume being purchased or annual spend for the incumbent product. Or your prospect may provide you with usage estimates. Whatever you learn can then be easily translated into potential for your product with simple math.

If you have received an RFP (Request For Proposal) the projected product volume and other key data points are typically provided in the document. This enables you to make an informed decision on how much business potential the RFP represents so you can make an informed decision and craft your response.

What if you do not have a clear and direct measure of potential? In those cases, proxy measures can help you establish potential. A proxy measure is another data point you can measure which then allows you to extrapolate potential based on how your product(s) and those data points correspond.

Another way to prioritize opportunities with greater revenue potential is to identify and focus on prospects with multiple product opportunities. Those opportunities can include the potential for a variety of products rather than one or a few, even if some of the product opportunities are future oriented, rather than current. Opportunities may include additional, broader product applications that lead to a greater volume of product usage.

The key strategy is to identify, confirm, and focus on qualified opportunities with the greatest new sales revenue potential. Also, increase the new sales revenue wherever possible by adding on additional opportunities or upselling opportunities when possible.

Application: Identifying and Prioritizing Revenue Potential

Factors for identifying and prioritizing the revenue potential of your sales opportunities are below. Check all factors that represent an opportunity to increase the dollar value of your sales opportunities.

Factors:

- ☐ Target analysis, identification, and prioritization.
    - o Analyze reports & resources.
    - o Utilize proxy measures where needed.
- ☐ Qualified opportunities.
- ☐ Quantified opportunities.
    - o Confirmed volume.
    - o RFP.
    - o Probing strategy.
- ☐ Additional product opportunities, including future product opportunities.
- ☐ Additional applications / utilization for existing products.
- ☐ Upsell opportunities and product mix.

Notes:

____

____

____

____

____

____

____

Higher revenue potential sales opportunities <u>Goals:</u> (what I am trying to achieve)

____

____

____

____

Higher revenue potential sales opportunities <u>Objectives</u>: (what I must accomplish to achieve my goals)

____

____

____

____

Higher revenue potential sales opportunities <u>Key Performance Indicators</u>: (how I will measure what I am achieving)

____

____

____

____

Higher revenue potential sales opportunities <u>Data, Reports, and Resources</u>: (information and tools I need)

____

____

____

____

Taking into consideration the factors essential to increasing the revenue potential of sales opportunities, and those factors that impact me most, my strategy to increase the revenue potential of my sales opportunities is:

____

____

____

____

____

____

____

____

____

Tactics – the <u>actions</u> I will take to increase the revenue potential of my sales opportunities include:

I will (action):   *by (timeline):*

____

____

____

____

____

____

____

____

____

SECTION 4: MAXIMIZING THE PILLARS OF SUCCESS

I first began accompanying other sales representatives on sales calls as a field sales trainer and then later as a Region Sales Manager and eventually as Vice President of Sales. I saw repeatedly that successful sales calls and successful professionals traced their roots to three key skill sets: 1) selling skills, 2) rapport and relationships, and 3) time/territory management.

These three areas of skill impacted success at the macro (territory) level on down to the granular results of each sales call. Success or failure could inevitably be traced to one or more of these "pillars of success."

Every sales professional must have a level of proficiency with selling skills to be effective. Effective sales professionals must manage their territory efficiently _and_ must be able to establish rapport and develop solid customer relationships. To the extent these skills are present and as they grow, so does the sales professional's effectiveness. However, if even one of the three Pillars of Success is substandard a sales professional will lack success.

Selling skills, territory management, and building relationships can all be very broad topics. Let's take each, in turn.

Section Goals

- **Maximize your selling skills**

- **Optimize time and territory management strategies**

- **Grow your professional relationships**

- **Enhance effectiveness through improved business acumen, product positioning, and self-management**

Chapter 22: Selling Skills

Selling skills are the communication and persuasive tools of our trade and are therefore vital to our success. While selling skills can and should be developed and honed throughout your career, it is not necessary to be an expert before you can be successful. However, there is a certain level of proficiency that must be achieved, or you will struggle. Selling skills include:

- Report and Data Analysis
- Observation
- Curiosity
- Investigation
- Probing / Probing Strategy
- Listening (Active and Critical)
- Product Presentation
- Product Demonstration
- Persuasion
- Influencing
- Overcoming Objections
- Gaining Commitment
- Motivating to Action

Which of the above are areas of strength for you? Which one(s) could be improved? Which selling skills are the ones you should be leveraging more?

When you consider your selling skills, there are two things to think about. Those two things are: how often and how well.

Consider a baseball player. We can all agree that baseball players do the same basic things whether they are a recreational player, high school player, college player, or a professional player.

All baseball players run, hit, catch, and throw, etc. But there is certainly a difference in skill level and proficiency.

That is true for sales professionals as well. Simply performing a skill does not necessarily mean that skill is done as often as it should be done. It also does not mean that skill is done well, or at the level that is required to be successful as a professional. So, as you evaluate your skills ask yourself if you are doing that skill as often as it needs to be done. Secondly, ask yourself if that skill is being performed at the professional level.

Feedback clarifies selling skills proficiency. There are two important sources of feedback that you should use to your advantage. The first source of feedback is your sales leader who can provide you with insights gained from work sessions, or meetings where they see you in action. A second source of feedback is your sales pipeline. As previously discussed, your pipeline directly reflects the results of your activities and the effectiveness of your selling skills.

Certain selling skills align strongly with uncovering sales opportunities and adding them as a qualified opportunity to your pipeline. Other selling skills come more into play as opportunities are cultivated and progressed through your selling cycle. Still, other selling skills are emphasized when closing the opportunity. By honestly assessing how well and consistently you build your pipeline, develop and progress opportunities through your pipeline, and your closing ratio you can identify strengths and opportunities for skills improvement.

For example, if you struggle to routinely add new opportunities, then you need to ask yourself if your focus and time allocation is as it should be, or if you have some associated skills that need attention. Selling skills that contribute to adding new opportunities include goal setting, reports, and data analysis, opportunity analysis, observation, investigation, probing, and listening.

Some constantly add new opportunities to their pipeline, but then those opportunities never seem to mature and close. Why is that? For some, the thrill of the hunt overshadows the discipline of follow-up and opportunity cultivation. Skills to examine in such instances may include goal setting, prioritizing, time and territory management, account management, building relationships, probing, listening, verbal and non-verbal communication, emotional intelligence, business acumen, needs development, solution identification, presenting solutions aligned to needs, goals, and wants, persuasion, objection handling, project management, and administrative skills.

Provided you have qualified the opportunity and advanced the opportunity to the cusp of closure, then barring unforeseen obstacles you should close most of your opportunities. If that is not the case, then what is holding you back?

Some sales professionals do not recognize purchasing signals when they occur. Others do not trial close so they cannot be confident that the customer is ready to commit. Still, others have a fear of asking for the decision or commitment, so they either fail to ask or their close is unassertive.

Some take the approach of "letting the product sell itself." That approach does not equate with true closing skills. This only works when the customer takes the lead and requests to purchase the product, so letting the product sell itself is entirely dependent on an assertive customer, which puts the onus and control in their hands. A sales professional should maintain control over the sales process and guide the selling conversation with fully developed selling skills.

Provided these are not the challenges that you face, other communication and closing skills may be the culprit. Those may include persuasion, gaining commitment, objection handling, or not fully uncovering all the customer's needs, goals, buying criteria, and wants. Probing strategy and listening skills may limit your ability to close successfully.

An often-overlooked skill is that of trial closing. Trial closing throughout the sales process confirms that you and your customer are progressing toward a successful conclusion together. Those who fail to trial close may be surprised when they do "pop the question" that the answer is "no." Somewhere along the way communication broke down and the discrepancy was never detected.

Lastly, your sales process may not end when the customer agrees to purchase. The product must still be shipped, received, and distributed for use. Without product utilization, your sale might as well not have occurred because you will not build sales revenue until product utilization occurs.

Product utilization requires the logistics mentioned to be worked out and in place. Product implementation and training may also be required before utilization occurs. If this describes your sales process, then the discipline and prioritization of follow-up and follow-through are vital to your success. Skills such as planning and coordination, communication, training, and education, along with customer service and support all are required. End-users must have the product readily available to them and they must be confident and competent in its use.

To the extent, product utilization lags expectations an analysis of the challenges and a plan of action must be created.

Application: Improve Your Selling Skills

The skills listed below are a representative list of selling skills. Add other selling skills where needed. Check all skills that represent a focal opportunity to improve your selling skills.

- ☐ Reports and Data Analysis
- ☐ Observation / Curiosity
- ☐ Investigation / Probing
- ☐ Listening (Active and Critical)
- ☐ Needs Analysis
- ☐ Product Positioning
- ☐ Presenting / Demonstrating
- ☐ Persuasion
- ☐ Influencing
- ☐ Cultivating the Opportunity
- ☐ Overcoming Objections
- ☐ Trial Closing / Closing
- ☐ Gaining Commitment
- ☐ Motivating to Action
- ☐ Driving Utilization
- ☐ Other: _______________

Notes:

____

____

____

____

Selling Skills <u>Goals:</u> (what I am trying to achieve)

____

____

____

____

____

Selling Skills <u>Objectives</u>: (what I must accomplish to achieve my goals)

____

____

____

____

Selling Skills <u>Key Performance Indicators</u>: (how I will measure what I am achieving)

____

____

____

____

Selling Skills <u>Data, Reports, and Resources</u>: (information and tools I need)

____

____

____

____

Taking into consideration the factors essential to good selling skills, and those factors that impact me most, my strategy to further develop my selling skills is:

____

____

____

____

____

____

____

____

Tactics – the <u>actions</u> I will take when I implement my selling skills improvement strategies include:

I will (action):   *by (timeline):*

____

____

____

____

____

____

____

____

____

____

Chapter 23: Time & Territory Management

Most sales professionals have a hard-wired bias for activity. That is a great attribute except when good activities commandeer our time and attention and prevent us from focusing on the best activities. Don't allow yourself to become too busy to be productive!

Effective time and territory management may be summarized as spending the right amount of time, on the right activities with the right customers. Your activities must be aligned to your goals and result in sales revenue growth that achieves your goals along with any other key deliverables that must be achieved.

Determining what effective time and territory management are for you then, must start with your goals. When you clearly define what you are trying to achieve (i.e., quota and any other key deliverables) you can then set your priorities to focus your time and attention on the actions that align with your goals.

A question you should constantly be asking yourself is "Of all the things I *can* do (this month, this week, today), which are the *most important* for me to do so that I reach my goal?" The answer is those activities that align with your goals, objectives, and strategies and are prioritized to enable you to achieve your goals. Time is not effectively used when it is spent on activities that are not aligned to your goals.

Your sales territory is defined geographically and by the existing and potential customers that reside within that geography. Customers, both existing and potential, can be further segregated according to those who can help you achieve your goals and those who cannot. A critical understanding is being able to accurately distinguish which category any given customer belongs to. Making the distinction begins with analysis and targeting as discussed in Goal-Based Selling Step One and is then confirmed when you qualify and quantify opportunities.

Your time is most productively spent on those customers who can (and will) help you achieve your goals. Key customers are members of that group. As we discussed earlier, key customers are those customers who, collectively provide at least 60 percent of your current base of business. When you examine the sales revenue contribution each key customer makes to your baseline sales you quickly realize you simply cannot afford to lose their business. Key customers may also present excellent growth opportunities. For these reasons, key customers require a certain portion of your time.

The other customers deserving of your time and attention are those customers who represent your best revenue growth opportunities. "Best" revenue growth opportunities are defined as those where your solution can meet the customer's needs and the opportunity can close quickly so that you can meet monthly and annual sales revenue growth goals (a qualified opportunity). And the opportunity has been confirmed to offer substantial revenue growth potential (the opportunity is quantified).

Such opportunities should be carefully and thoughtfully analyzed. Because of the time and attention, each opportunity requires to navigate and develop, you can only effectively manage a certain number of them simultaneously. In a complex sales environment (one with multiple decision influencers and decision-makers) developing opportunities often requires you to spend significant time interacting and communicating with many people within the organization.

Servicing key customers and developing growth opportunities will require the bulk of your time. And, you will still have other miscellaneous activities that take time here and there. The key to effectively managing your time and territory is to determine exactly how much time you will dedicate to key customers, prospective growth opportunities, and other activities. Then, you must practice self-control and discipline in following your time allocation.

The practical side of territory management is travel to and from customer locations. To minimize time wasted in travel, plot on a map the location of those customers with whom you will spend most of your time. If necessary, use one of the many software tools that are available to efficiently route travel. This kind of technology will benefit you by saving you time.

By setting appointments, pre-planning the meeting including meeting outcome goals, and creating meeting agendas you will further reduce wasted time. Although in-person meetings are preferred, consider when other means of communication will be effective yet timesaving.

Application: Improve Time and Territory Management Skills

Check all factors that represent an opportunity to improve your time and territory management skills.

Factors:

- ☐ Goals and priorities dictate activities.
- ☐ Strategic Plan is in place and followed daily.
- ☐ Efficient territory routing & travel.
- ☐ Appropriate time allocation between key customers, prospective customers, and priority activities.
- ☐ Key customers are identified.
- ☐ Thorough account management.
- ☐ Appropriate level of customer service & support activities.
- ☐ New customer development.
- ☐ Maximizing the value of current customers.
- ☐ Leveraging appointments vs. drop in.
- ☐ Meetings have agendas and outcome goals.
- ☐ Other:_______________________________

Notes:

____

____

____

____

____

____

____

Time and Territory Management <u>Goals:</u> (what I am trying to achieve)

____

____

____

____

____

Time and Territory Management <u>Objectives</u>: (what I must accomplish to achieve my goals)

____

____

____

____

____

Time and Territory Management <u>Key Performance Indicators</u>: (how I will measure what I am achieving)

____

____

____

____

Time and Territory Management <u>Data, Reports, and Resources</u>: (information and tools I need)

____

____

____

____

Taking into consideration the factors essential to good time and territory management skills, and those factors that impact me most, my strategy to further develop my time and territory management skills is:

____

____

____

____

____

____

____

____

Tactics – the <u>actions</u> I will take when I implement my time and territory management skills improvement strategies include:

I will (action):   *by (timeline):*

____

____

____

____

____

____

____

____

Chapter 24: Rapport & Relationships

The importance of rapport and relationship-building skills cannot be overstated. An old truism is "all things being equal, friends do business with friends. And all things being not so equal, friends still do business with friends." Since relationships are so important let's define the nature of the relationships that we're seeking.

You may be familiar with the phrase Bob Burg coined: "know, like, and trust." Those three words aptly describe the nature of a good business relationship and can serve as a benchmark of how your customers should feel toward you. At a minimum, customers should know who you are as a professional, they should like who you are as a professional, and they should trust you as someone they are willing to do business with. Relationships are easy to establish when customers know you hold their interest as a priority and when you can be counted on to "do the right thing."

The establishment of a positive business relationship can occur relatively quickly, even as quickly as during the initial meeting. By professionally presenting yourself, as an open and approachable person who demonstrates knowledge, competency, and a genuine interest in learning about your customers, meeting their needs, and helping them to achieve their goals, you will establish a relationship that is conducive to business.

As your professional demeanor and actions continue to reinforce your customer's perception of you the relationship can continue to grow and develop. When you bring measurable value to your customer and when you have solidified in their mind that you are someone they truly enjoy working with and benefit from doing business with, you can begin to earn the status of being a trusted resource and advisor.

All that was just described was in the context of a business relationship because mutual business interests are the origin of and reason why the relationship exists in most cases. While business relationships can and do grow into genuine personal friendships as well, the important thing to remember is that good business practices and professionalism will always be at the center of a good business relationship.

Good business relationships enable and facilitate business, but relationships will not last long if they are not consistently earned and reinforced. Don't take your valued business relationships for granted. Your best customers and best business relationships are your competitor's biggest targets.

Business relationships are vital to your success, but they are not an end unto themselves. Some sales professionals primarily seek to build relationships and then they expect the relationship to be the reason that their customer does business with them.

Though it is true that "friends do business with friends" it is all the other aspects of good selling that should be the reasons that any customer does business with you. In other words, you bring value to them by providing the right solution to their problem, and/or you help them achieve their goals. Your customers should want to do business with you because you are professional, worthy of the trust they put in you, and because you provide them superior customer service and support. The relationship facilitates business, but it cannot be the sole reason for doing business.

On the other hand, I have seen a few sales professionals who struggle with selling to customers with whom they have strong business relationships. They stop selling and pursuing new growth opportunities with those customers because they feel they are putting the relationship at risk by doing so.

If you find yourself also dealing with this conundrum, stop and consider the value that you providing to your customers. Are you solving a problem, helping them succeed in their aspirations, and helping them achieve their goals? Are you providing superior service? Are you fair with your pricing and your business practices?

When I have seen sales professionals struggle with selling to their customer friends it is usually because they somehow feel like they are "pushing" a product or service they don't feel good about or they are conducting business in a manner that is not consistent with their values.

If it is true that you are providing a valuable solution, a superior level of service, and doing business in an honorable way then you should have no qualms selling to your very closest business friends. You are helping them succeed and you should feel great about that. But if the opposite is true and something is lacking then you should correct whatever is at the root of your concern. Business relationships will quickly be destroyed by a lack of trust if a customer feels they are being slighted or taken advantage of.

The skills that go into establishing and growing strong business relationships involve probing and listening. Good manners and emotional intelligence play important roles as well. If you want others to know you, be knowable. If you want others to like you, be likable. If you want others to trust you, be trustworthy. Respect the other person. When you request time with them ensure there is purpose and value that is evident for them. None of this should be surprising, it is all the attitudes and attributes we have been taught since we were children. The key is living them out.

Because we tend to like others who are like us, practices such as "mirroring" are often very effective in establishing a comfort level quickly. That is, we mirror their behaviors and communicate similarly. If they are loose and relaxed, then we mirror that in our body language. If they are more reserved and business-like then we are as well. If they speak slowly and thoughtfully and are mild in tone, then that is how we should communicate, too.

The goal of mirroring is not to be obvious in copying the other person, which could become annoying to the other person if they realize that is what you are doing. Instead, it is to behave in like fashion to create a comfortable and familiar atmosphere that is conducive to a productive conversation. By mirroring we can help to minimize differences that could otherwise detract from our conversation.

Application: Improve Rapport and Relationship Skills

Check all factors that represent an opportunity to improve your rapport and relationship skills.

Factors:

- ☐ Likable
- ☐ Friendly
- ☐ Courteous
- ☐ Trustworthy
- ☐ Professional Demeanor
- ☐ Builds Trust
- ☐ Trusted Advisor
- ☐ Identify Decision Makers / Influencers
- ☐ CRM Management
- ☐ Listening Skills
- ☐ Emotional Intelligence
- ☐ Mirroring
- ☐ Attitude

Notes:

____

____

____

____

____

____

Rapport and Relationships Skills <u>Goals:</u> (what I am trying to achieve)

____

____

____

____

Rapport and Relationships Skills <u>Objectives</u>: (what I must accomplish to achieve my goals)

____

____

____

____

Rapport and Relationships Skills <u>Key Performance Indicators</u>: (how I will measure what I am achieving)

____

____

____

____

Rapport and Relationships Skills <u>Data, Reports, and Resources</u>: (information and tools I need)

____

____

____

____

Taking into consideration the factors essential to good rapport and relationship skills, and those factors that impact me most, my strategy to further develop my rapport and relationship skills is:

____

____

____

____

____

____

____

____

Tactics – the <u>actions</u> I will take when I implement my rapport and relationship skills improvement strategies include:

I will (action):   *by (timeline):*

____

____

____

____

____

____

____

____

Chapter 25: Business Acumen

The term business acumen gets thrown around quite a bit, but the definition is not always clear. If you are a bit unclear on the definition, do not worry, you are not alone! Even amongst the 'experts', business acumen definitions differ slightly.

Let us bring some clarity and start with defining **acumen**. Merriam Webster defines acumen as "keenness and depth of perception, discernment, or discrimination, especially in practical matters."[11]

The Oxford Learner's Dictionaries defines acumen as the "ability to understand and decide things quickly and well."[12]

By combining both definitions, we might say that acumen is keenness and depth of perception, discernment, or discrimination especially in practical matters resulting in the ability to understand and decide things quickly and well.

Acumen, then, applies to a variety of functional areas. For example, sports fans may ascribe a high football acumen to a player who is deeply knowledgeable, smart, and crafty. A high baseball acumen may describe a coach who develops better game plans and outmaneuvers other coaches.

Since our focus is business, let us create a working definition for business acumen. **Business acumen** is keenness and depth of perception, discernment, or discrimination especially in *business* matters that results in the ability to understand *business* and decide things quickly and well. Business acumen can be further described as understanding the impact on business (now) and the implications (future) of the decision on the business.

---

[11] Merriam-Webster. (n.d.). *Definition of acumen*. Retrieved Feb. 2, 2022, from: https://www.merriam-webster.com/dictionary/acumen
[12] Oxford Learner's Dictionaries. (n.d.). *Acumen noun*. Retrieved Feb. 2, 2022, from: https://www.oxfordlearnersdictionaries.com/us/definition/american_english/acumen

We might also say a person has "business sense" or "business savvy," when talking about individuals who possess strong business acumen. We would say that those with strong business acumen display "keen insights," and are "shrewd" business professionals.

According to the Perth Leadership Institute, "Business acumen is based primarily on behavioral and experiential issues, not on formal learning or education like financial literacy."[13]

Dr. Ray Reilly and Dr. Greg Reilly indicated "developing stronger business acumen means a more thoughtful analysis, clearer logic underlying business decisions, closer attention to key dimensions of implementation and operation, and more disciplined performance management."[14]

Finally, Chris Berger said that "business acumen starts with the ability to understand how a company makes decisions, and that leaders must be financially literate and be able to understand numbers on company financial statements. It entails the ability to take the knowledge of business fundamentals and use it to think strategically and then take appropriate action."[15]

Every professional can enhance their business acumen by knowing what business acumen is and how it is developed. Growing business acumen is a career-long endeavor and using it wisely provides a distinct advantage.

A linear progression of building business acumen is as follows: <u>knowledge</u> leads to <u>understanding</u>, which leads to <u>decision making</u>, which leads to <u>actions & behaviors</u>, which leads to <u>outcomes</u>, which leads to corporate <u>achievement and success</u>.

Business acumen may be summarized in three words: knowledge, understanding, and implications. By combining knowledge, understanding, and implications, you can make sound business decisions. Your effectiveness is enhanced so you can be a more productive and valued

---

[13] Perth Leadership Institute. (2008, Jun.). *The Role of Business Acumen in Leadership Development (Updated and Reissued)*. Retrieved from: https://www.perthleadership.org/documents/Business_Acumen_WP_Updated.pdf

[14] Reilly, R.R. & Reilly, G.P. (2009, Dec.). *Building Business Acumen: What it is, why it's important and how to get it*. HR West.

[15] Hastings, R.R. (2008, Apr.). *Business Acumen Involves More Than Numbers*. SHRM.

member of your organization. You can sell more effectively due to your greater credibility, insights, and your capacity to create "win/win" scenarios.

Business Acumen and Your Organization

As a sales professional, you have a unique role within your organization. You have a direct impact on revenue generation and profitability. Because you directly interact with customers, you are a vital conduit of information between your organization and theirs. You acquire new customers and build loyalty with existing customers. Each of these abilities means you can bring tremendous value to your organization.

To perform at your maximum capacity and deliver the greatest value to your company you must have a deep understanding of how your organization makes money and profit. Know your organization's goals and priorities and how you impact the departments within your organization.

Business Acumen and Your Customer

You and your products have a profound impact on your customers and their ability to achieve their goals. You may help them perform their job more effectively. Your product(s) may improve financial performance via increased efficiencies, or your product may help them better satisfy their customers.

The more you know and understand your customer's business model along with their goals and priorities, the more you can bring value and thus earn their business. You will sell your products more effectively because you can position them effectively and help your customers understand the benefit to their business. This ability elevates you above competitive representatives who simply push a product without understanding broader implications on the customer's business and goals.

When considering how you can bring value to your customers recall that people buy your **product**, your **company,** and **YOU**! Any of these alone, or in combination can provide unique value that earns the customer's business. The key is knowing what those unique values are and then effectively communicating how they benefit your customer's business.

Business Acumen and Your Industry

Knowing and understanding your industry is also a key part of your overall business acumen. That is because industry trends may present opportunities or threats that can affect your company or your customers, independent of their actions or plans.

For example, if the price of coffee beans skyrockets, it impacts everyone from Starbucks to the cool little independent coffee shop down the street, and your local grocery store. If you want coffee, it is going to cost you more, regardless of your source. That is because the price of coffee beans is fundamental to the business model of anyone selling coffee.

Fortunately, there has never been a time in history where information was as readily available as it is today. By tapping into those information sources, you can stay abreast of industry news and trends.

I trust that by now the benefits of strong business acumen are apparent. The benefits are numerous for you as an employee and as a sales professional. Now is the time to commit to continuous learning and development so that you maximize your business acumen, personal effectiveness, performance, and value.

The first step in your journey should be the decision to commit to ongoing learning and development. Set your goal for building business acumen. Set your goal, identify your objectives, create your strategy, and take action with tactics that are goal-driven and in line with your strategy.

Application: Improve Your Business Acumen

Check all factors that represent an opportunity to improve your business acumen.

- ☐ I possess a keenness and depth of perception, discernment, or discrimination especially in business matters.
- ☐ I make good business judgments and quick business decisions.
- ☐ I understand the impact and implications of the decisions on my business.
- ☐ I understand my organization's business and the impact and implications of decisions on my organization's business.
- ☐ I understand my customer's business and the impact and implications of decisions on my customer's business.
- ☐ Growing business acumen is a goal for me and will continue to be a career-long endeavor.
- ☐ I understand my industry, stay abreast of industry trends, and know the implications of those trends for my business and my customer's business.
- ☐ My business acumen separates me from my competition, providing me with a distinct competitive advantage.

Notes:

____

____

____

____

____

____

Business Acumen <u>Goals:</u> (what I am trying to achieve)

____

____

____

____

____

Business Acumen <u>Objectives</u>: (what I must accomplish to achieve my goals)

____

____

____

____

____

Business Acumen <u>Key Performance Indicators</u>: (how I will measure what I am achieving)

____

____

____

____

____

Business Acumen <u>Data, Reports, and Resources</u>: (information and tools I need)

____

____

____

____

____

Taking into consideration the factors essential for business acumen, and those factors that impact me most, my strategy to further develop my business acumen is:

____

____

____

____

____

____

____

Tactics – the <u>actions</u> I will take when I implement my business acumen improvement strategies include:

I will (action):   *by (timeline):*

____

____

____

____

____

____

____

____

____

Chapter 26: Product Knowledge and Positioning

Product training and product knowledge are paramount to your ability to sell effectively. Before you begin working with customers in your territory you most likely went through extensive product training. Perhaps you continue to receive ongoing periodic product training as well.

In your corporate product training, you learn all the key features, benefits, and advantages that pertain to your product and for competing products, too. And while that training and knowledge is valuable, there are other aspects of product knowledge you need to be aware of to maximize your credibility and effectiveness. You need to understand your product and competitor products from a real-world, third-party point of view as well. This aids your ability to be credible when speaking with current and prospective customers.

To quickly gain real-world product knowledge and understand the market, customer needs, customer attitudes, and hands-on product performance, learn directly from your customers. Go to high-volume customers and interview them. If possible, do a preceptorship where you shadow them and vicariously live "a day in the life" of your customer.

To be clear, your purpose is not to engage in any form of selling during the interview or preceptorship. You are there strictly to observe, listen, and learn. What is it that caused your customers to select and purchase your product when they did? What other choices were they considering, if any? What "tips and tricks" have they learned along the way to enhance product performance or have the product better meet their needs? What are the parameters for use where your product performs at its best and shines? What challenges do they encounter when using your product? Learn all that you can so that you are well equipped with real-world product use information in addition to the classroom training you received.

As you learn more about your product and its competitors, you will better understand that properly positioning the product is key. All products and services perform at their best and provide the most benefit when used within certain parameters and according to realistic expectations.

Problems occur when those parameters or customer expectations are exceeded. Your goal in building your product knowledge is to know exactly what the parameters are for your product to perform its best. Learn what the expectations should be for your product so that when customers evaluate and use your product they will be thrilled with its performance. If you want to sell a product most effectively, position it well.

Many organizations include in their product training an overt or underlying message that their product is superior to all other competing products. They want to instill within you that the product is "the best" within its class, bar none. The organization's goal is to give you confidence in the product. But be aware, there can be dangers lurking in the concept of "better" and "best."

Make no mistake, where your product has unique qualities and benefits, you should highlight them, demonstrate them, and exploit them. Your customers should be made aware of when, why, and how your product distinguishes itself from its competitors.

But what if your product is essentially similar to competitors in function and outcomes? Can you still sell it effectively? If you allow yourself to be objective, don't be surprised to find that the differences between products (yours and competitors) can be minimal. Perhaps the differences are even seen by customers as negligible. That scenario can be especially challenging if you are a sales professional who thinks their product must be "the best" to sell it effectively. Relax and remember that it's all in the positioning.

Some sales professionals spend a lot of time and effort trying to convince customers their solution is indeed the best and superior to all others. This approach can serve to undermine their credibility and success when customers know that is not the case.

A better approach is to understand exactly what the customer needs and why. Then, position your product properly within the parameters and expectations where it performs best. Show customers that your product will meet their needs and expectations. If you do this, you will be able to successfully sell your product without having to prove it is "the best."

As an example, let us pretend you sell automobiles. Pick your favorite premium brand and pretend that is the one you represent. I think we can all agree that in today's market there are many excellent domestic and foreign choices. There are examples of premium brands that are rooted in the latest new technology and others that provide fantastic traditional technologies. The point is, while your specific brand may indeed provide an excellent option, other brands may be considered just as good, or even better, to the customer who prefers one technology or feature set versus another.

So then, how do you distinguish and effectively sell your automobile? Just as in any other selling scenario you discover what your customer wants, needs, and prefers. You uncover as much information as possible so that you can then position your car and present it in its best light. Most importantly, you let the customer experience your offering and convince themselves that it is what they want.

On more than one occasion in my past, I represented products that were indistinguishable in performance when compared to their competition. I knew this and my customers also held that conviction. Because the products all yielded such similar results, it was frustrating to customers when the various sales representatives tried to highlight and distinguish their products as the singular best choice. The results simply did not bear out any differences.

In selling those products I never tried to convince my customers that my product was "the best." That would be a fruitless exercise… What I did instead was to probe and get to the root of why customers would select one product over another. Then, I would use the rationale they provided and position my product accordingly.

In one example, customers spread their product selection amongst the competitive options equally. They did this out of a desire to be "fair" to the competitors. At that time there were two main competitors, so customers split their business roughly 50/50 between them.

When I encountered these customers, I explained to them why my product would produce results that were at least comparable to what they were currently getting from the competitive products.

Since they desired to be "fair" in using the two market leading products, would they now be willing to divide their business into thirds so they could be "fair" and use my product in the mix as well? Many times, they would consider this question for a minute and then indicate their willingness to do just that.

In another case, I was tasked with launching a new product that competed in a very tough, long-established market. Independent testing proved every competitive product worked extremely well – as did the product I represented. Once again, my goal in selling the product was not to convince the customer that mine was "better" or "best" because that was not realistic. Instead, my strategy was focused on having my product be the first product selected when the need arose.

My approach was simple. I would walk my customer over to the selection of products and ask them what caused them to pick one up first instead of the others. Most customers responded by saying whatever product they had more of would be their first selection. I simply had to ensure my customers had more of my product than any others.

In those cases, I knew my product would perform as expected. I knew it would meet, and often exceed the customer's expectations. After the customer had seen my product perform, I could then present the distinguishing features that caused my product to perform as well as it did. They believed me when I presented those distinguishing features because they had seen it work. On the other hand, I was met with skepticism by customers who had not yet seen my product perform.

In both cases I used the customer's reasoning and current practices to position my product. After the product had proven its effectiveness, I could then "sell" the benefits and unique features that enabled my product to perform so well and further cement their loyalty to me and to my product.

When customers are highly skeptical of anything you might claim initially (though it is true), once they experience your product and see it produce the desired results their skepticism begins to dissolve. It is replaced by a willingness to learn the reasons behind your product's performance.

This is your opportunity to solidify the sale and ensure your customer is now a full-fledged supporter as opposed to the cynical and jaded customer you originally met.

All of this is made possible when you understand the most important aspects of product knowledge. That includes all the products that comprise your market and how they compare. It includes knowing what the typical customer behaviors, attitudes, and beliefs are relative to your product and the competitive products. And being willing to ask the questions that reveal customer rational and reasons why without tripping yourself by pushing facts and figures that won't be believed anyway – at least until after your customer has experienced your product.

What are the technical and practical attributes that enable your product to perform at its best? And what are the circumstances in which it performs at its best? What customer expectations does your product meet and exceed?

You must have a deep understanding of these factors so that you know how to position your product appropriately and advantageously. You must know where your product shines and where it does not.

Let us revisit our automobile sales example. While it is fun to sell the "best" product on the market, realize that many more customers purchase mid-level and even entry-level automobiles. Given the choice, would every consumer love to have "the best?" Sure, they would! Can everyone afford "the best?" No.

The point is that every product has a customer base with a matching set of purchasing criteria. As a sales professional, you can sell a lot of products that may not be the market-leading pinnacle product. By positioning the right product to the right customer everyone wins.

In fact, "the best" can be defined in many ways by different customers. Some may consider the latest technology to be the best while others prefer the simplicity and less problematic nature of older, more proven technology. Some prefer the highest quality regardless of price while others prefer the value of good quality at a lower price. In their mind overall value is "the best."

So, as sales professionals, we need to use caution in using "ER" and "EST" when describing our products. That is, in using superlatives such as stronger, faster, higher, better, or best. Any superlative that we use in describing our product might be disputed by customers if their definition of the chosen superlative does not apply in the same way. What can happen is that customers get defensive over the superlative in question and the conversation degrades from there.

A better approach is to understand things from your customer's perspective. Understand your customer's definition of better and best and how such terms apply to your products or competitive products. Then, position your product appropriately and focus on the sale at hand.

Lastly, recall that we previously discussed that customers buy three things: your product, your organization, and you! Each of those can provide unique benefits and value to your customer. Each should be appropriately positioned within the overall value proposition you present your customer.

Application: Improve Your Product Knowledge and Positioning

Check all factors that represent an opportunity to improve your product knowledge.

Factors:

☐ Know the Market:

- Understand market dynamics and drivers.
- Understand competitive landscape.
- Understand how each product fits within the market.
- Understand customer perceptions and attitudes.

☐ Know Your Product:

- Be objective and realistic.
- Technical aspects.
- Practical aspects.
- Best application - where does <u>my</u> product shine?
- Best positioning.

☐ Know the Competitive Products:

- Technical aspects.
- Practical aspects.
- Best application - where does <u>their</u> product shine?

☐ Understand "ER"/"EST" through your customer's eyes.

☐ Understand, and when appropriate, use the customer's rationale.

☐ Maximize your value proposition according to the unique benefits your product provides, your organization provides, and the benefits you provide.

Product Knowledge <u>Goals:</u> (what I am trying to achieve)

____

____

____

____

____

Product Knowledge <u>Objectives</u>: (what I must accomplish to achieve my goals)

____

____

____

____

Product Knowledge <u>Key Performance Indicators</u>: (how I will measure what I am achieving)

____

____

____

____

Product Knowledge <u>Data, Reports, and Resources:</u> (information and tools I need)

____

____

____

____

Taking into consideration the factors essential to increasing my product knowledge, and those factors that impact me most, my strategy to increasing my product knowledge is:

____

____

____

____

____

____

____

____

Tactics – the <u>actions</u> I will take to increase my product knowledge include:

I will (action):   *by (timeline):*

____

____

____

____

____

____

____

____

____

____

____

Chapter 27: Coachability and Self-Management

Being coachable means you choose to engage others and allow them to help guide you. In business, the manager/employee relationship tends to be thought of in terms of a reporting structure. While that is certainly accurate, it does not readily convey the same type of relationship that a professional athlete has with their coach.

The professional athlete/coach relationship evokes the notion of mentoring and helping the other to maximize performance. The athlete and coach collaborate to sharpen strengths and minimize weaknesses. They strategize and implement game plans that result in a shared victory when they succeed as a team.

The professional athlete and the sales professional share many common characteristics. They both compete against others who are highly motivated, highly trained, and intent on winning. For sales professionals, it is more productive to embrace sales leadership as a coaching-oriented relationship than simply a reporting structure.

A coaching relationship implies common goals, objectives, and strategies. A coaching relationship also implies that you, as the sales professional, are willing to seek and implement coaching. Communicate frequently with your coach. Align yourself to organizational goals, strategies, and priorities and be a good team member.

A healthy coach/professional relationship is built on trust and open communication. At times you will see things differently than your leadership. That is normal and you should be able to have a healthy and positive debate. But when it comes time to execute the game plan do it wholeheartedly, with a laser focus, and with vigor! When you act, do so with a sense of urgency. Seek to get the most productivity out of each day that you possibly can.

Along with being coachable, strong self-management is essential because sales professionals typically operate independently more than any other function in an organization. Accordingly, sales professionals must be tough-minded and resilient. It is necessary to actively manage morale and energy because every customer must get the best version of you every time. That requires energy, persistence, and fortitude! A positive, gracious, and professional attitude does not magically overcome us during working hours, we must cultivate that attitude and be determined to maintain it.

How, then, do we do that? First, choose to present the best version of yourself every day. Be willing to be accountable. By proactively taking responsibility you can overcome any temptation to take on a victim mentality. Those who take on a victim mentality rob themselves of their ability to problem-solve and create change. Victims are helpless and sales professionals cannot afford to be helpless at any time.

Also, be wary of conversations with the Negative Nellies. Every organization seems to have that person or group who ruminates on every negative thing. If there isn't something worthy of fear, uncertainty, and doubt they will dig until they find it, or easier yet, just make it up! Don't spend time talking with them or they will quickly drag you down to the mire in which they love to wallow. Before you know it, you will be miserable too! That misery comes at a real cost: the cost of performing at your best and eventually, the cost of commission and bonus dollars. Nobody can sell effectively when their attitude is poor. Not only are they not able to think clearly and give their best effort, but customers can sense negativity and it is a huge turn-off.

Have you noticed the times I used the word "choose" and how I have positioned your attitude as a choice? It is because you decide how you will comport yourself. You can be proactive in seeking feedback, being timely, being courteous, focused on priorities rather than distractions, and so on. As you take control of your attitude you take control of your ability to be successful. As the popular phrase goes, just do it! And the more you do it the easier it will become.

Application: Improve Your Coachability and Self-Management

Check all factors that if adopted or practiced more often, will improve your coachability and self-management.

Factors:

- ☐ Teachable
- ☐ Proactively takes direction
- ☐ Seeks and implements coaching
- ☐ Accepts and takes responsibility
- ☐ Actively manages moral and energy
- ☐ Proactively accountable
- ☐ Open communication
- ☐ Self-motivated
- ☐ Self-disciplined
- ☐ Focused
- ☐ Acts with a sense of urgency
- ☐ Other:____

Notes:

____

____

____

____

____

Coachability and Self-Management <u>Goals:</u> (what I am trying to achieve)

____

____

____

____

____

Coachability and Self-Management <u>Objectives</u>: (what I must accomplish to achieve my goals)

____

____

____

____

____

Coachability and Self-Management <u>Key Performance Indicators</u>: (how I will measure what I am achieving)

____

____

____

____

Coachability and Self-Management <u>Data, Reports, and Resources</u>: (information and tools I need)

____

____

____

____

____

Taking into consideration the factors essential to my coachability and self-management, and those factors that impact me most, my strategy to increase my coachability and self-management is:

____

____

____

____

____

____

____

____

Tactics – the <u>actions</u> *I will take to increase my coachability and self-management include:*

I will (action):   *by (timeline):*

____

____

____

____

____

____

____

____

____

Chapter 28: The Mental Side of Selling

As a sales professional you know selling is a high-pressure, highly individualistic, and competitive pursuit. You know the ever-present stress your quota and strategic initiatives create. You spend most of your time in the field with prospects and customers, who can be challenging and downright difficult at times. It can feel quite isolating since your support network is not just across the hall or at the nearest water cooler, which may be the case for others who work in a more typical office environment.

Sales organizations can have hundreds or even thousands of sales professionals. Each of those professionals represents internal competition because you are constantly vying for top performance rankings. Externally, competitive representatives are trying their best to take your customers away and steal your deals.

The world of professional selling is not for the faint of heart. You must be mentally strong and resilient. You must develop your mental skills just as surely as you must hone and polish any other professional skill. Professional selling is a thinking person's game.

If it's Meant to be its Up to Me

Your mindset is vital to your success. Recognize and embrace the importance of taking responsibility and being proactively accountable. You are the star of a one-person show. Yes, there are many supporting characters but, in the end, you are in the driver's seat, and you control your destiny. When you take ownership of your goals, plans, actions, and performance, you will be on the road to success.

Put the Odds of Success in Your Favor

You will have peaks and valleys, wins and losses. Such highs and lows are inevitable. The key is to put the odds of success in your favor so that you enjoy many more wins and peaks. You put the odds of success in your favor by doing all that we have talked about in **Selling Smarter**. Set your goals and create your plans. Execute your plans with energy, enthusiasm, and diligence. These actions all rely on mental discipline – *your* mental discipline - to complete them. Putting the odds of success in your favor begins in your mind. You must first decide, and then commit before any of the actions will ever take place.

Anxiety, Insecurities, and Confidence

As sales professionals, it is important to project a sense of confidence in ourselves, in our products, and in our organization. However, sometimes we face feelings of anxiety or insecurity. "Faking it until you make it" is not a viable option because it's not authentic, and those we interact with will know something is amiss. Furthermore, even if you can fake it for a while, there is no guarantee that these anxieties or insecurities will magically vanish overnight. They must be understood and faced.

If something is making you feel anxious, take the time to understand why. A way to do this is to take a similar approach as the root cause analysis that we discussed in Section 2: How to Get Back on Track When There's a Gap. Once you have clarity on the root cause, you can determine the appropriate steps to begin overcoming anxiety and insecurities.

A big cause of anxiety is a lack of preparedness. On the other hand, being fully prepared creates a sense of confidence. Preparation may include learning new information, creating a meeting agenda, anticipating key points to be discussed, practicing a presentation or demonstration, etc. Take time to consider what is making you anxious or insecure, then target your energy into filling any gaps in your preparation.

Prior successes also create confidence. When you have encountered similar situations and navigated them victoriously you will feel more confident as a result. If there is something you find especially challenging, don't avoid it because avoidance only feeds insecurity and doubts. Instead, accept that you may or may not 'win' but by tackling head on that which intimidates you, it will be a learning experience that pays dividends going forward.

Prior success does not have to be your own experience. Others who have experiences and successes can help you understand the requirements and nuances you have not yet experienced. Seek out those who can help you and ask, listen, and learn!

How to Fail Well

Failure is not something anyone wants to encounter, especially in a professional setting. Understand that it's okay to fail at something. We all do, and we all have. The important thing is to learn and improve.

There are two types of failure. 'Good' failure is failure you can learn from and ultimately benefit from by having gone through the experience.

Thomas Edison is known as saying, "But the student will find that experience is the best teacher. The reason why I get along with comparative ease now is because I know from experience the enormous number of things that won't work. For instance, I start on a new invention tomorrow. From the great number of experiments I have made, and the vast amount of information I have stored up, I am saved a great deal of time and trouble in not having to travel over barren ground."

Failure is only negative when it results from something we could have and should have been able to avoid, such as by being more prepared, working harder, or any other action within our control.

How to Overcome a Bad Day

Let's say the worst has happened. You failed badly. You could have and should have avoided failure, but it occurred anyway. How do you recover and move forward?

Going back to a previous comment, the place to start is by recognizing and embracing the importance of responsibility and accountability. Be proactive. Don't wait for your customer, peer, or boss to initiate a discussion with you. Is there a way to right the wrong? Do it!

When you do encounter losses take the time to reflect on what happened and why. Taking responsible steps to ensure that you will never again fail in the same way for the same reasons shows maturity and professionalism.

On the other hand, let's say the worst has not happened. But it has been a negative situation. In short, you had a bad day! Again, the productive approach is to acknowledge what happened and reflect on why it happened. Was the situation within your ability to control? If so, determine how can you avoid a similar situation going forward and enjoy a better outcome. Focus your attention on the adjustments or improvements that are needed and how you will implement them. You will have more positive energy and a healthier outlook if you do this rather than simply lamenting poor results.

What if the situation was outside of your control? If there was nothing you could have done to avoid or prevent the unpleasantry, then it's an opportunity to further develop your resilience. Think of all the appropriate clichés such as, "What doesn't kill me makes me stronger," or "Pain is weakness leaving the body." I'm not suggesting you make light of the situation, but I am suggesting that you don't take it personally or let the negativity linger and further affect you. Let it go and move on.

What you may find is that taking a professional approach to difficult situations can provide you with unique opportunities. I have experienced a customer taking out their frustration on me and then, at a later date, they apologized profusely. By being professional initially, I was able to connect with them at a deeper level and have a more honest and open conversation about their business. Also, often people feel like they "owe you one" and will be more open about exploring opportunities for business.

Managing Mental Energy and a Positive Outlook

Managing your mental energy and outlook are every bit as valuable as other resources you manage such as your time, focus, and budget. If you are not positive and energized, you will not be able to perform at your highest level.

Negative conversations drain our mental energy and can create a negative outlook. I'm not talking about challenging conversations with customers, I'm talking about the conversations we engage in voluntarily with friends or peers. Other drains on our mental energy include procrastination, lack of discipline, distractions, and other related activities. Be determined and take control of your own behaviors when such temptations present themselves. Don't allow yourself to become mired in those mud holes. You must protect your mental energy and outlook.

Focus instead on your goals and what must be done to accomplish them. Focus on the attentions and activities you know to be productive. Invest your time and energies in your own success. By doing so you will be putting the odds of success in your favor, you will be more productive, and your outlook will be improved.

Dealing with F.U.D.

Fear, uncertainty, and doubt = F.U.D. It is not rational, but it can still get to us. The first step in dealing with F.U.D. is to avoid the sources of F.U.D. If you have been infected with F.U.D., it can be helpful to write out what is causing your feelings of F.U.D. Writing makes you think through all the details in order to write them down. Once you have everything on paper you can take a long look at what you wrote down and decide if your concern is logical or illogical. Probable or improbable. What would have to happen for your F.U.D. to come true? What is the likelihood those things will occur?

In my corporate career, I have heard all manner of rumors and worrisome comments. The vast majority of rumors and worries never came to be. Let me repeat that: they NEVER came to be! Meanwhile, the time and energy wasted on worrying and discussing "what-if scenarios" was always real. I'll bet if you think through your experiences, you will find the same to be true. The moral of the story is, don't waste your time on F.U.D. It only bogs you down and by the time you realize your fears were unfounded, you will have wasted substantial time and mental energy. Just say no!

More Fears and Ways to Overcome Them

I have also seen situations where sales professionals became frozen or intimidated due to the importance of the customer and the meeting at hand. When the moment starts to feel too big, stop and realize that your well-conceived plan and practiced approach will help you succeed. If you have prepared well, then you have reason to look forward with anticipation. Trust in your preparation!

Another situation I experienced was representatives, and even sales managers, who were afraid to take what would otherwise be normal steps to advance business opportunities. The fear was in being too forceful or too aggressive and thus offending the customer. Inevitably, these situations arose with prospective customers who represented large potential, but at the time did little or no business with the sales professional in question. It seemed the possibility that the prospective customer would someday want to do business was more attractive than the reality of taking the actions and confirming there was or was not a qualified opportunity.

If you have experienced such situations, you must have the courage to move forward as you would normally. Qualify and cultivate the opportunity. Don't let the fear of losing a vague and undefined sale cause you to waste time and focus. It is much better to qualify the opportunity and know with certainty that you can develop and close it, or, to know with certainty that there is no real opportunity so that you can focus elsewhere.

"No" is Not "No" Forever

Many sales professionals want to avoid "no" because they think it is a permanent decision. Sometimes that is true. Many other times, however, "no" is "no" for now, but not "no" forever. When you realize this truism, you can more confidently attempt to close when the time is right to do so.

There are times that you might lose an opportunity to a competitor. If you know the customer will not ultimately be satisfied with the product they have chosen, follow up and attempt to win them over. If you give up at "no", then you will miss sales that you would have otherwise been able to win with some patience and persistence. In such cases, your mindset must be focused on a longer time horizon and your determination must overcome your initial disappointment in missing the opportunity the first time around.

The Physical Side of Mental Health

How you feel impacts how you think. When you are not healthy, fit, or energized your mental state will suffer. To be in the best frame of mind, to think clearly and to have the right attitude, you must do what is necessary to support good physical condition. Eat right, exercise, and get the right amount of rest.

Take a page from the books of top athletes. They know that in order to perform at their best, they must train physically. To a large extent, selling can be physically demanding and mentally demanding. Performing and competing effectively requires the same sort of diligence in maintaining a good physical condition.

Application: The Mental Side of Selling

Below are the factors essential to an effective sales mentality. Check all factors that, if improved, would positively impact your mentality.

Factors:

- ☐ Use mental strength and resiliency.
- ☐ Dismiss anxiety and insecurities that hinder my success.
- ☐ Be proactively accountable and taking responsibility for my actions.
- ☐ Identify root causes of failures so that I learn from them and do not repeat them .
- ☐ Avoid becoming bogged down by bad experiences beyond my control.
- ☐ Proactively manage my mental energy as I do other valuable resources.
- ☐ Do not allow procrastination, lack of discipline, distractions, or other related activities to drain my mental energy.
- ☐ Do not allow F.U.D. to steal my time and focus.
- ☐ Plan, prepare, and practice so that I perform at my best regardless of how high the stakes are.
- ☐ Courageously do what I know is needed to qualify opportunities and move them forward.
- ☐ Realize that "no" is not "no" forever. When needed, leverage determination over time to win opportunities.
- ☐ Manage my physical fitness, including my diet, exercise, and rest to support my best and most positive mental fitness.

What would enable you to make your sales mentality even more effective?

____

____

____

____

Sales Mentality <u>Goals:</u> (what I am trying to achieve)

____

____

____

____

____

Sales Mentality <u>Objectives:</u> (what I must accomplish to achieve my goals)

____

____

____

____

____

Sales Mentality <u>Key Performance Indicators:</u> (how I will measure what I am achieving)

____

____

____

____

____

Sales Mentality <u>Data, Reports, and Resources:</u> (information and tools I need)

____

____

____

____

____

Taking into consideration the factors essential to an effective sales mentality, and those factors that impact me most, I will improve my sales mentality by:

____

____

____

____

____

____

____

Tactics – the <u>actions</u> I will take to improve my sales mentality include:

I will (action):   *by (timeline):*

____

____

____

____

____

____

____

Chapter 29: Compete to Win!

When I was a field sales trainer, I was asked to work with a salesman who was struggling. We spent a few days working together and I could not find any obvious reason for his lack of performance. He seemed to have all the skills, knowledge and attributes needed to succeed yet he was struggling.

Then on one of our last sales calls together he made a comment that suddenly raised a huge red flag for me. We were discussing a competitor that we faced, and he said, "I don't get why there has to be so much animosity, my attitude is live and let live."

Right then I knew what the issue was. While he might harbor a "live and let live" attitude, I was certain that his competitors did not. They were out for blood, and he was suffering because of it. He had no willingness to compete at all and it showed in his numbers.

As sales professionals, we and our competitors do not stand on opposite sides of our customers and verbally go back and forth until someone wins the business. But in another sense, that is exactly what is happening though we're not all present in the same room at the same time. There is a constant battle for the business, and you are always competing for your customer's attention and business. How then, do we put our best foot forward and compete most successfully?

Start by reviewing who you are as a competitor. What are your strengths and opportunities for improvement? How are you most effective and what can you do better? Analyze yourself to gain insights into how you can compete most effectively. Leverage your strengths and minimize any weaknesses.

Analyze who you compete against. Individuals have distinct styles and preferences, strengths, weaknesses, and reputations within the industry. You can learn a lot about a competitor you never meet in person just by speaking with customers and listening to how they describe your competitor. Also, use the online resources available to learn about those who represent competitor organizations. Learn as much as you can about your competitors, especially those who you encounter most frequently, those who are most successful, and those who are newly entering your market and are a possible new threat.

This advice applies to competitive organizations as well as their representatives. Organizations have a collective personality that is evidenced by their marketing methods and messages. Check out their website to see how they present themselves. There may be a news section on their website that provides access to stories and announcements. And some websites tout prominent customers or new products in development or products that are about to be launched. That is always good information to have.

Organizations gain reputations based on their business practices and you should be very familiar with the business practices and the reputation of those you compete against. As we discussed earlier, while some products may be hard to distinguish from their competition, organizational business practices may provide you with the advantage you seek. Are competitors seen as easy or difficult for customers to work with? Are their contracts one-sided and onerous? What about their terms and conditions or warranties and returns? What is their reputation for quality? There are many points of potential distinction that can provide you a vital advantage if you do your homework and know your competitors inside and out.

To assist in performing an analysis, you can utilize a simple tool: a S.W.O.T. Analysis. Analysis can be performed on nearly anything including yourself, a competitive organization, a competitive product, etc. To perform a S.W.O.T. Analysis you list all strengths, weaknesses, opportunities, and threats that pertain to your subject. While the exercise is simple, and it can yield some great insights. It is especially powerful when done in a group setting because so much input can be provided and discussed.

Subject of S.W.O.T. Analysis: ____

Strengths:	Weaknesses:
Opportunities:	**Threats:**

To compete effectively you need a plan. Create your goal, objectives, strategies, and tactics designed specifically to overcome challenges and capture those opportunities that most impact your ability to compete successfully.

Being in highly competitive environments can be taxing. This is where personal motivation and a strong sense of determination come into play. You are going to encounter some difficulties and you won't win them all. By cultivating resiliency, knowing your competition, having a plan, and utilizing some creativity you can compete successfully.

When facing a strong competitor, it can be challenging and it's not always possible to win all the business in one fell swoop. In such cases, and if the nature of your product or service is conducive to the strategy you may consider the approach of incrementalism.

The strategy of incrementalism is summarized as finding a starting point that enables you to gain a foothold of business with a customer. Then, you incrementally expand and grow your business with that custom by ensuring the product performs as expected, developing your relationships with the key individual(s), continuing to learn as much about their business as possible so that you consistently grow by solving additional problems or helping them to achieve additional goals. Through product performance, business acumen, service and support, and a persistent growth mindset you can incrementally grow your business.

An example of incrementalism is becoming a secondary supplier. For any company that operates in a highly dynamic environment and especially considering the severe supply issues, we have seen there is a rationale to secure a secondary supplier to minimize any disruption.

If you are unable to win the primary supplier position, then a secondary supplier position is better than none. And you can employ the strategy of incrementalism to earn and eventually take over as the primary supplier. You do this by outperforming and outcompeting the primary supplier daily.

In selling and business, competition will always be a fact of life. What works today won't necessarily work tomorrow because market conditions change, new products come to market, and organizations switch tactics. To compete effectively over time, you must periodically stop and assess. Do routine S.W.O.T. analysis. Review your competitors regularly. Stay abreast of market conditions that may impact you, your customers, and your competition. Adjust your plans as needed so that you are always in your strongest position to win in the arena in which you compete.

Application: Improve Your Ability to Compete and Win!

Check all factors that if performed or improved, will improve your ability to compete successfully.

Factors:

- ☐ Identity: Who are you…and who is your competitor?
- ☐ Competes vigorously.
- ☐ Competes within the rules and laws of professionalism.
- ☐ Conducts SWOT analysis.
- ☐ Presents skills and abilities.
- ☐ Shows up prepared.
- ☐ Determines clear goals.
- ☐ Aligns priorities and actions with goals.
- ☐ Creates and executes a strategic sales plan.
- ☐ Adept at finding a starting point.
- ☐ Practices incrementalism.
- ☐ Shows determination.
- ☐ Motivates themselves.
- ☐ Engages in self-reflection to assess and adjust.

Notes:

____

____

____

____

____

____

Compete! <u>Goals:</u> (what I am trying to achieve)

____

____

____

____

Compete! <u>Objectives:</u> (what I must accomplish to achieve my goals)

____

____

____

____

Compete! <u>Key Performance Indicators:</u> (how I will measure what I am achieving)

____

____

____

____

Compete! <u>Data, Reports, and Resources:</u> (information and tools I need)

____

____

____

____

Taking into consideration the factors essential to my ability to compete, and those factors that impact me most, my strategy to competing more effectively is:

____

____

____

____

____

____

____

____

Tactics – the <u>actions</u> I will take to increase my ability to compete include:

I will (action):   *by (timeline):*

____

____

____

____

____

____

____

____

____

____

Chapter 30: Put It All Together – My Keys to Success

Congratulations on your effort and good work! You are way ahead of the game since most sales professionals do not go to the trouble of creating a detailed, written plan as you have done. By completing this Playbook, you have already begun to distance yourself from the competition and put yourself solidly on the path to a successful sales campaign.

According to an April 2018 Forbes article: "Vividly describing your goals in **written** form is strongly associated with goal **success**, and people who very vividly describe or picture their goals are anywhere from 1.2 to 1.4 times more likely to accomplish their goals than people who don't."[16]

Similarly, a January 2019 Inc. Magazine article summarized the research of Psychology professor Dr. Gail Matthews. Her study found goal achievement in the workplace was influenced by three key actions: **"writing goals, committing to goal-directed actions, and lastly, creating accountability for those actions."** By doing these three things, study participants were able to escalate their success rate up to 76%![17]

Through the course of creating your Playbook, you've already completed the first two key actions, which were 1) writing your goals and 2) committing to goal-directed actions. The third key component is to "create accountability for those actions."

---

[16] Murphy, M. (2018, **Apr. 15**). *Neuroscience Explains Why You Need To Write Down Your Goals If You Actually Want To Achieve Them*. Forbes. Retrieved from: https://www.forbes.com/sites/markmurphy/2018/04/15/neuroscience-explains-why-you-need-to-write-down-your-goals-if-you-actually-want-to-achieve-them/?sh=599bddbe7905

[17] Gardner, S. & Albee, D., (2015). *Study focuses on strategies for achieving goals, resolutions*. Dominican University of California. Retrieved from: https://scholar.dominican.edu/news-releases/266

Upon completing your Playbook meet with your sales manager and review your Playbook together. Focus on your Goals and Action Plans. Then, agree to an accountability process so that you will provide yourself the greatest possible benefit from all the work and thoughtful planning you've invested in your success. Once done, you're on your way to raising your likelihood of achieving your goals and quota between 20% to 76%!

Application: My Strategic Plan

Your last Playbook exercise is to take a few minutes to review this workbook from the beginning. Review your notes and the strategic plans you have created. Make any updates you want to capture. Now, while everything is fresh in your mind, on the following page you will distill everything into what is ***most important*** to your success as you move forward. This will be your personalized, focused plan for success. Succinctly answer the following questions by summarizing your previously recorded detailed notes and plans. Do not exceed the space given for your responses.

My keys to protecting key customers and the revenue they generate:

____

____

____

____

My keys to sales revenue growth:

____

____

____

____

My keys to an effective pricing strategy:

____

____

____

____

____

My keys to achieving quota:

____

____

____

____

My keys to maximizing my skills, abilities, strategies, and attitude:

____

____

____

____

My Prioritized 3 Keys to Success Are:

1)____

2)____

3)____

I will create an accountability process with:

____

ABOUT THE AUTHOR

Kevin Onarecker developed, trained, and led high-performing sales teams for 23 years. As VP of Sales, his teams were recognized by customers as best in class. The revenue growth generated under his leadership was a key element in a successful exit.

As Regional Sales Manager, Kevin's teams were top achievers many times. His innovative sales strategies were adopted and implemented organizationally. Numerous team members emerged as leaders who today continue to lead successful teams of their own.

As a sales professional, Kevin distinguished himself with awards for top performance. He knows a great deal about professional selling and what is required to achieve success. The contents of *Selling Smarter* were derived from years of real-world, professional selling and thousands of sales calls.

Kevin has been married for over 30 years to the love of his life, Shasta. They have a son and daughter who have enjoyed academic success and are soon to launch their own careers.

To feed his competitive side, Kevin plays a variety of sports including flag football, tennis, and softball. Recently, he has taken up pickleball as well. To relax, he enjoys camping, hiking, and exploring national parks with his family.

Selling Smarter is based on training sessions and workshops designed by Kevin to get results. Goal-based selling training courses include goal-based selling process, work smarter to hit your goals, back on track, business acumen for sales professionals, selling for the small business, and optimizing your sales team. To learn more about Kevin's business, Onarecker Consulting, Inc., please visit www.onareckerconsulting.com.

REVIEWS

"This is not a book you simply read, but that you can actually use to improve your performance. Kevin has done a great job incorporating best practices and examples for all the advice provided. The worksheets will guide you through the process as if he was sitting right next to you. I highly recommend this book for anyone in sales. Whether you are new to selling or a seasoned professional, you will benefit from the insights provided."

Vince Burruano, President, Vince Burruano Consulting Services, LLC

"The thing that keeps sales managers up at night is making sure that EVERY team member reporting to them has a firm grasp of the task at hand: to achieve the territory sales goal of quota achievement. It is the crucial step in the beginning of the fiscal year and throughout the year that can determine income, achievement, and recognition. A sales rep with a sound territory plan and foundation will enjoy their year and not be stressed by falling behind or being scrutinized more closely for subpar performance. EVERY sales rep should want a beautiful and sustainable '4-bedroom house every year' using the G.O.S.T. method."

Andre Cotrufello, 40 Years of Medical Sales Management, Marketing, and Sales Experience

"I loved reading **Selling Smarter** by Kevin Onarecker and recommend the book with its extensive library of guides and forms to my clients that want to improve sales performance. I've built multiple sales teams and sales operations in companies ranging from start-ups to those valued in the billions, and I learned a lot reading the book. It's perfect for ambitious salespeople, business owners, and sales operations people that want a step-by-step guide on how to plan and execute sales success."

Charlie Janes, Certified FocalPoint Business and Executive Coach

"This is an outstanding distillation of the sales process that leads to success! There is no fluff here. Any enterprising sales professional can find the keys to achieving and exceeding annual sales goals by following the direction set forth in this book. Tapping into his outstanding sales career, Kevin has been able to directly and accurately lay out the map for accomplishing regular sales achievement. You would need a library of sales books in order to boil down the wisdom, direction, insight, and tips contained in this one book. This is a great tool for sales professionals and those that manage them!"

Craig Schweers, District/Regional Sales Team Leader in Pharma and Biotech

"Congratulations! With this book you are one step closer to achieving your quota. Kevin Onarecker has put a one-of-a-kind playbook together that turns meeting and exceeding your quota into an easy-to-follow, step-by-step process. Read, complete, and succeed."

Henning Schwinum, Co-Founder & Managing Partner, Vendux LLC

APPENDIX 1: TEMPLATES

Pipeline Opportunities > 75% Confidence

Pipeline Opportunities ≥ 75% Confidence

Name	Close Month	1X Sales Revenue	Periodic Sales Revenue	Number of Periods	CY Periodic Sales Revenue	Total Sales Revenue
Example 1	February	$1,000	$1,500	10	$15,000	$16,000
Example 2	June	$0	$750	6	$4,500	$4,500
Example 3	September	$5,000	$2,500	3	$7,500	$12,500
Totals:		**$6,000**			**$27,000**	**$33,000**

Pipeline Opportunities ≥ 75% Confidence

Name	Close Month	1X Sales Revenue	Periodic Sales Revenue	Number of Periods	CY Periodic Sales Revenue	Total Sales Revenue
Totals						

Rule of 78s Positive and Negative Carry Forward – Examples and Templates

Rule of 78s is an especially useful tool for sales professionals selling products that generate revenue monthly or at frequent, regular intervals throughout the year. In other words, when a new customer is closed, they can be expected to purchase your product monthly or at least regularly and routinely going forward.

See the example below. In this case, the customer began purchasing in March, so net growth over baseline sales will occur over the next 12 months. If your sales year is a calendar year, then you will realize 10 months of sales growth from this customer and then two months of your next sales year will benefit from "carry forward." You will have two months (and the associated dollars) of sales you may expect due to the close that occurred in the prior sales year.

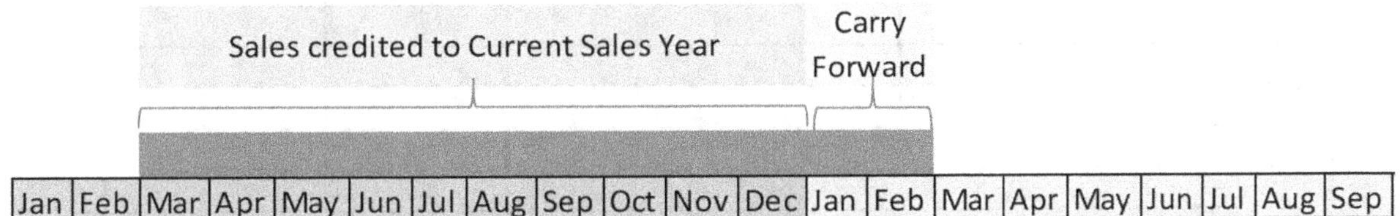

While this example is for new business, which provides a positive impact going forward, the reverse situation occurs when a customer is lost. In that case, whatever monthly sales were generated by the customer will NOT occur going forward, so over twelve months, you will have a monthly negative impact of lost sales. Just like new business carries forward, any lost accounts that stop purchasing within your current sales year will hurt the next sales year.

Rule of 78s - Projected Positive Carry Forward into CY

Name	PY Close Month	Periodic Sales Revenue	Number of Projected CY Periods	Projected Carry Forward Sales Revenue
Example 1	February	$1,500	2	$3,000
Example 2	June	$750	6	$4,500
Example 3	September	$2,500	9	$22,500

Totals: **$30,000**

Rule of 78s - Projected Positive Carry Forward into CY

Name	PY Close Month	Periodic Sales Revenue	Number of Projected CY Periods	Projected Carry Forward Sales Revenue

Totals:

Rule of 78s - Projected Negative Carry Forward into CY

Name	PY Lost Month	Periodic Sales Revenue	Number of Projected CY Periods	Projected (-) Carry Forward Sales Revenue
Example 1	February	$1,250	2.00	$2,500
Example 2	June	$500	6.00	$3,000
Example 3	September	$3,500	9.00	$31,500
			Totals:	$37,000

Rule of 78s - Projected Negative Carry Forward into CY

Name	PY Close Month	Periodic Sales Revenue	Number of Projected CY Periods	Projected (-) Carry Forward Sales Revenue
			Totals:	

Course Correction Worksheet

Annual Quota   (1) $________________

Baseline Sales   (2) $________________

Growth Objective (New Sales Revenue)   (3) $________________   Original Goals

Monthly Closes Goal (Original):

- One-time Sales
  (Original Growth Objective / 12)   (4) $________________
- Recurring Sales
  (Original Growth Objective / 78)   (5) $________________

YTD New Sales Revenue (Result of New Closes)   (6) $________________

Avg Mo. New Rev (YTD New Sales Rev / Months)   (7) $________________

YTD Growth Objective (–) YTD New Sales Rev.   (8) $________________   Current State

YTD Baseline Sales (Current Customers)   (9) $________________

YTD Baseline Sales (Annualized)   (10) $________________

Current Quota Gap (Quota – YTD Sales)   (11) $________________

Monthly New Sales Revenue Goal (Revised)   (12) $________________

*For recurring sales use Rule of 78s

**factor lost recurring sales for lost customers   Revised Goals

Pipeline Goals:

Monthly   (13) $________________

To Achieve Quota   (14) $________________

APPENDIX 2: GLOSSARY

Baseline Sales: The total sales revenue from the prior fiscal year. Baseline sales are measured at the customer level, territory level, and on up to the organizational level.

Current Year (CY): refers to the current fiscal year.

Decision Influencers: stakeholders who do not have the authority to finalize the decision to purchase your product but who can influence the decision maker.

Decision Makers: those stakeholders who have the authority to finalize the decision to purchase your product.

End-Users: those who use and work with your product or service in their daily activities.

Farmer: Farmers are those who focus on growing sales by developing existing customers.

Goal-Based Selling (GBS): is the process of identifying and using goals to guide every facet of what we do as sales professionals. The GBS Sales Process provides a sequential pathway beginning with opportunity identification, qualifying and quantifying the opportunity, developing a mutual understanding of customer needs, presenting and demonstrating the solution, gaining a product evaluation (if needed), gaining commitment, then closing the sale and implementing the product.

Growth Objective: the difference between quota and baseline sales. *See also The Quota Equation (below).

Growth over Prior Year: a comparison of sales revenue performance compared to the prior year. Common comparisons are for the current month versus the same month last year, the current quarter versus the same quarter last year, the current YTD versus YTD last year, and the current year versus last year.

Hunter: Hunters are those who are more focused on proactively and aggressively seeking out new customer opportunities.

Key Performance Indicators (KPIs): strategic data points that measure results and confirm whether the associated goal is being achieved.

Net Growth Objective: the sales revenue growth calculated to achieve quota taking into account baseline sales rate of growth or decline.

Performance Improvement Plan (PIP): A PIP is implemented when performance is not meeting expectations and will usually result in termination of employment if the specified goals are not achieved. The PIP is administered by sales management with guidance from Human Resources and Senior Sales Management. A PIP specifies goals and KPIs that must be achieved within a specific timeframe, typically between thirty and ninety days.

Prior Year (PY): refers to the prior fiscal year.

Quota: the annual sales revenue goal that is assigned to each sales territory. Quotas typically have quarterly goals as well.

Request For Proposal (RFP): an RFP is issued to suppliers and potential suppliers when a purchasing organization is seeking to acquire a product or contract for a product. The RFP will stipulate specific information to be provided.

Rule of 78s: for a recurring revenue model, the Rule of 78s provides a means of calculating how much new recurring revenue must be generated to achieve a year-end revenue goal. The Rule of 78s gets its name due to the 78 purchasing periods that occur over a 12-month period. As the year progresses, the number of periods remaining decreases as each month goes by.

The Rule of 78s calculation is YTD Growth Objective $____________ / (number of periods remaining) = Monthly New Sales Revenue Goal $_____________

Run Rate: run rate extrapolates sales from a period and projects an annual total. A common run rate measure is the three-month run rate. In this measure, the average revenue from three months is projected to a 12-month total. Month A + Month B + Month C = $X. $X/3 = monthly average. $X 12 = projected annualized sales.

Sales Pipeline: A list of qualified prospective new business opportunities. Important details minimally include the account name, the product(s), the potential new revenue volume, and expected close date.

Sales Trend: the rate at which sales revenues are growing or declining over time. Sales trends may be measured for any period of time, but three month and twelve-month trends are common measures.

Stakeholders: those in your organization (internal stakeholders) or customer organizations (external stakeholders) who are involved with or impacted by your product or service.

The Quota Equation: Baseline Sales + Growth Objective = Quota. Or, said another way, Quota – Baseline Sales = Growth Objective.

Year Over Year (YOY): a comparison of the current fiscal year to the prior fiscal year. This may be expressed in percent change or in dollars.